THE WISEST FOOL
And Other Men of the Bible

The
WISEST FOOL
And Other Men of the Bible

By

CLARENCE EDWARD MACARTNEY

MINISTER, FIRST PRESBYTERIAN CHURCH
PITTSBURGH, PENNSYLVANIA

ABINGDON-COKESBURY PRESS
NEW YORK • NASHVILLE

THE WISEST FOOL

SET UP, PRINTED, AND BOUND BY THE
PARTHENON PRESS, AT NASHVILLE,
TENNESSEE, UNITED STATES OF AMERICA

FOREWORD

Including those in this book, I find that I have preached 167 sermons on the characters of the Bible. In a number of instances, however, some of the sermons have dealt with different aspects of the same men and women, or with different incidents in their lives. It has been a long and delightful study for me. I discovered early in my ministry that people like biography; and nowhere is there such biography, so stirring, so moving, so uplifting, so tragic, as that to be found in the Bible.

It has been a joy to me to learn that these different volumes of sermons on Bible characters have been suggestive and of help to not a few preachers in their own work and ministry. There are still other interesting men and women in the Bible about whom I have never preached a sermon. Perhaps at some time in the future I shall be able to preach on them also.

Clarence Edward Macartney

CONTENTS

I

SOLOMON—THE WISEST FOOL IN THE BIBLE

"Solomon in all his glory."

MATT. 6:29

"Every man the plague of his own heart."

I KINGS 8:38

KING JAMES I OF ENGLAND, WHO ALSO REIGNED AS JAMES VI of Scotland, was the son of Mary, Queen of Scots. He was the king to whom our "authorized" King James Version of the Bible was dedicated, but hardly worthy of the high praise bestowed upon him in that dedication, which speaks of his "many singular and extraordinary graces." King James had, however, some literary taste, and wrote a number of works. When James broke with France and made an alliance with Spain, Henry IV of France in a famous sentence described him as "the wisest fool in Christendom."

Solomon may well be described as the wisest fool in the Bible. Christ spoke of "Solomon in all his glory." There was no doubt about that glory. God made Solomon the touchstone of human splendor and glory. But in the end all this glory came to nought. Solomon casts one of the longest shadows in the Bible and in history. His architecture, engineering works, his knowledge, wisdom, riches, splendor, proverbs, and poems have become a tradition. We know much about the outside life and splendor of Solomon; and yet we cannot say that we know him in the way we know Joseph, Moses, Samuel, Elijah, Peter,

[9]

John, or Paul. So much is this so that at the end of his history we are not sure where to place Solomon, whether among the kings who did that which was right in the sight of the Lord, or among those who did that which was evil in the sight of the Lord.

SOLOMON'S YOUTH AND CHOICE

Solomon was the son of Bathsheba, with whom David sinned. If Absalom, who brought so much anguish and sorrow into his father's life, had been the son of Bathsheba, we would have termed it poetic justice and retribution. But it was Solomon who was the son of Bathsheba. Bathsheba was as ambitious for Solomon's future and splendor as she was beautiful in person and in body. As a youth Solomon was given into the custody and tutelage of the great prophet Nathan, who rebuked David for his sin with Bathsheba. When David was on his deathbed it was the wisdom and enterprise and ambition of Bathsheba which secured the throne for Solomon, when David's other son, Adonijah, conspired to seize it.

Shortly after this David slept with his fathers; but before his death he spoke a great farewell message to Solomon. In that farewell message David said: "I go the way of all the earth." How true that is! There are some people who never get very far from the place where they were born. They are contented with home scenes and early surroundings. Others again have crossed the seas and continents in search of new homes and new fortunes. And still others, filled with the spirit of unrest, have wandered to and fro and up and down in this earth. But traveled or untraveled, rich or poor, wise or foolish, there is one journey which at length, at the appointed time, every man must take. It is the journey that David was about to take when he said: "I go the way of all the earth." And of all the memorable things said concerning death by philosophers, kings, peasants, prophets, apostles, nothing is so appropriate, so comprehensive, so adequate as that saying of David: "I go the way of all the earth."

It was a great charge that David gave to Solomon. "I go the way of all the earth," he said to Solomon. And then what? In view of the fact that death would soon end his life and take the scepter from his brow, and the sword of authority from his hand, and still forever his marvelous harp of poetry and of song, what did David say? Did he say to his son: "Solomon, there is nothing in life. This, my son, is what you will come to after you have ruled and reigned and conquered. Life is only a tumult, a vain show"? No! That was not what David said. What he said was this: "Be thou strong therefore, and show thyself a man; and keep the charge of the Lord thy God, to walk in his ways, to keep his statutes, and his commandments, and his judgments, and his testimonies." That is the real test. After the pilgrimages, the storms, the battles, the disillusionments, the temptations, the transgressions, the hopes, the joys, the trials and sufferings of life, then what does the man have to say of life? Will he say what David's son said at the end: "Vanity of vanities"? Or will he say what David said to Solomon: "Life is a great and noble and honorable experience. Therefore be strong and show thyself a man"?

No man ever started better or with greater promise than Solomon. At Gibeon his coronation was celebrated with tremendous hecatombs of burnt offerings. Gibeon was the place where the tabernacle and the ark were lodged, and where the altar had been built by Bezaleel 450 years before. Now the sacrifices are over; the rejoicing throngs who shouted, "God save the king!" have departed. In the silence of the night the stars come out—the same stars which sang together at the creation of the world. That night God appeared unto Solomon in a dream and said to him: "Ask what I shall give thee." There were no reservations, no exceptions. "Ask what I shall give thee."

Let us see what Solomon did *not* ask for. He did not ask for wealth and gold and silver. The ancient world set great store by gold. To them it was the symbol of splendor. They traced their chariots with gold, covered their ceilings with gold, embossed their shields with gold. They ate from golden plates, slept on golden couches, and lighted their candles in golden candelabra. They quaffed their wine from golden goblets and drew their swords from golden scabbards. Gold! Gold! Gold! Multitudes, then as today, asked to choose what they will have, would have chosen gold. Yet Solomon did not ask for gold.

Neither did he ask for vengeance on his enemies. Ancient coronations began with the music of proscription and massacre. But Solomon did not ask for revenge on his enemies. Neither did he ask for victory in battle over hostile kingdoms. He did not ask for splendid palaces, or for world renown, a name which would ring throughout all the earth. Neither did he ask for long life. Long life was esteemed a great blessing in the Old Testament age. The psalmist cherishes the promise: "With long life will I satisfy him, and show him my salvation." To come to one's grave in a full age was regarded as a special mark of the divine favor. A long life was treasured more than it is today, probably because the hope of immortality was dimmer then than it is today. Yet Solomon did not ask for long life.

For what did he ask? He asked for an understanding

heart. This is what he said to God that night: "I am but a little child: I know not how to go out or come in. . . . Give therefore thy servant an understanding heart to judge thy people, that I may discern between good and bad: for who is able to judge this day thy so great a people?"

Twenty-eight hundred years afterward, on June 20, 1837, a blue-eyed eighteen-year-old girl in England was awakened at six o'clock in the morning by the archbishop of Canterbury and the lord chamberlain of England, who told her that her uncle King William IV was dead and that she was Queen of England and the dominions beyond the seas. Then the lord chamberlain opened the Bible to the third chapter of First Kings and read to her the story of Solomon's choice. Twenty-nine hundred years afterward, the vice-president of the United States, chatting and joking with his friends at the Capitol, was summoned to the White House, where he was told that the four-times elected president was dead, and that he was now elevated to the august office of the presidency in the most critical and awful day the world had ever seen. The next day, addressing the Congress, he took the nation to his heart and won universal approval by concluding his address with the prayer of Solomon: "I am but a little child: I know not how to go out or come in. . . . Give therefore thy servant an understanding heart to judge thy people, that I may discern between good and bad: for who is able to judge this thy so great a people?"

"Ask what I shall give thee!" Solomon is not the only one to whom God appears in a dream and says: "Ask what thou wilt." Every young man has his own Gibeon. Solomon asked for wisdom, the power to choose right as against evil, and for an opportunity to use that wisdom and power for the good of others. He did not ask for a long life, but for a good life, a life long in its influence for good upon others.

> We live in deeds, not years, in thoughts, not breaths;
> In feelings, not in figures on a dial.
> We should count time by heart-throbs. He most lives
> Who thinks most—feels the noblest—acts the best.[1]

In the famous story of the Choice of Hercules, Hercules, at the turning of the road, was confronted by two maidens. One, in gaudy attire and with wanton looks, asked him to follow her, promising that if he did so he would have every delight and pleasure that life could afford. But the other, in plain attire and modest of demeanor, said to Hercules: "I shall not deceive you. The path that I point out is full of labor, full of trials, full of difficulties; but it is a path that leads to immortality. If you seek to be beloved by your friends you must serve your friends. If you desire to be honored by any city you must benefit that city. If you wish to be admired by all Greece for your merit you must endeavor to be of service to all Greece." And her name was Virtue. O mystic night of dreaming and of choice! Ask what thou wilt! There is a common saying: "He asked for it and he got it." But this is true more than just in the sense of retribution. Life has its frustrations, its disappointments; but, so far as the inner life is concerned, by the grace of God we can have that for which we ask.

> Thou hast a choice. To choose is to create.
> Remember whose the sacred lips that tell.
> Angels approve thee when thy choice is well.[2]

[1] Philip James Bailey, *Festus*.
[2] Longfellow.

THE GLORY OF SOLOMON

God made Solomon the touchstone of human splendor and glory. He did not ask for gold and riches; and yet it came to him in such abundance that he made silver and gold to be in Jerusalem as stones. He did not ask for palaces, but God gave him the House in the Wood, with the great ivory throne overlaid with gold, and its walls hung with the shields of gold. He did not ask for earthly knowledge, but God made him the wisest man of his age. He was the author of three thousand proverbs, which are still the measure of human wisdom, and a thousand and five songs. He was a naturalist who knew all the flowers and trees and plants, from the cedar of Lebanon to the hyssop that springeth out the wall.

> That warrior sage, whose restless mind
> Through nature's mazes wandered unconfined;
> Who every bird and beast and insect knew,
> And spake of every plant that quaffs the dew.

Solomon did not ask for empire, but God gave him a kingdom that stretched from the river unto the ends of the earth. "The kings of Tarshish and of the isles shall bring presents: the kings of Sheba and Seba shall offer gifts."

The climax of Solomon's glory was the temple of Jehovah. That beautiful building, erected in humble loyalty to his father and to the glory of God, has long since passed away. Its courts and porches, the two great pillars Jachin and Boaz with the lily work on them, the molten sea on the backs of the twelve oxen, the cherubim and the seraphim, the pomegranates, the great crimson veil, the holy of holies, and the ark of the covenant—all that has completely passed away. But the prayer that Solomon offered at the dedication of the temple still remains—not a stone missing, not an altar of its confession and supplication overturned, not a pinnacle of its aspiration broken. Eloquent and sublime token of the survival of the Spirit and of the things of the Spirit over the things made with hands!

SOLOMON'S FALL

God made three special appearances unto Solomon: first, when he appeared to him at Gibeon and asked him to choose what he would have; second, when he appeared to him in the midst of his glory and splendor to warn him; and finally, when he appeared unto him to condemn him and judge him.

When Solomon was in the midst of his glory and splendor, and his name was ringing throughout the world, God appeared a second time to him. The Lord renewed the promise given him before, but also warned him that if he forsook the statutes of God and served other gods, the great temple that he had dedicated would become a hissing and a byword in the earth. From this we judge that Solomon was beginning to waver, and that already there were signs of deviation from the path of honor and righteousness. This prepares us for the third appearance of God to Solomon, to condemn him and to judge him. The fair morning and the glorious midday of Solomon's life have faded into the darkness of midnight. God comes to tell him that because his heart has turned away from God, who had appeared unto him twice, his kingdom will be rent from him.

What lies back of this amazing fall? Solomon's fall was in a way stranger and more shocking than that of

David himself. David as an idolator is unthinkable. David's fall was the passion and impulse of the moment. But the fall of Solomon was the slow crumbling and disintegration of a great character. The king whose youthful desire was to do good to his nation became an oppressor, and God raised up adversaries against him, such as Jeroboam, upon whom the aged king sought to lay a murderous hand. The king who dedicated the temple of Jehovah with his sublime prayer built idols for the worship of the heathen gods, and bent his aged knees at the altars of the gods of his heathen wives. This is the Bible's epitaph on Solomon: "His wives turned away his heart after other gods."

What a fall is this! Who is this we see oppressing the people with grinding taxes, building altars for licentious Ashtoreth, Chemosh, and Molech in the very precincts of the temple of Jehovah? Who is this who now seeks to murder his ministers? Who is this who chooses chariots and horses and foreign wives and concubines? Alas, it is Solomon! That same youth whom we saw kneeling there in the starlight by the altar of Gibeon and asking God for the wisdom of righteousness and faith! Truly none fell from higher pinnacle of glory to a deeper abyss of sin and shame. He illustrates the truth of the saying of the ancient Spartan philosopher: "Count no man happy until the end."

It is not enough to dream well, to ask for great things. Great dreams and great requests call for great loyalty. A biographer said of Francis Bacon, who sold himself to the corrupt and ignominious government of James I: "No one ever had a greater idea what he was made for; but he was not true to what he knew." Likewise Solomon. None ever had a greater idea of what he was made for.

None ever chose more wisely in his youth the Kingdom of God and his righteousness. Yet none ever fell from a greater height to a deeper depth. He dreamed well, but he was not faithful to his dream.

The Arabs have a legend of how a worm was silently, invisibly, eating out the heart of a staff upon which Solomon leaned. Whenever you try to live without God, whatever your wisdom, power, fame may be, listen! You can hear the gnawing of that secret worm! But we need no Arab legend to tell us that. Solomon himself proclaimed it in the unforgettable phrase of his great prayer at the dedication of the temple, when he spoke of how prayer and supplication might be made there by any man which shall know the plague of his own heart.

"Every man the plague of his own heart!" That is what the world denies, scoffs at, ignores, and yet at the same time is forever and sadly illustrating and demonstrating. Yes, every man has that plague—the plague of sin in his own heart. That was the secret of Solomon's ruin and fall. It is the enemy within against which we must be ever on our guard. And it was to deliver us from the power and blight and condemnation of that plague within that Christ came and suffered and died for us. He alone can conquer that plague. "The blood of Jesus Christ his Son cleanseth us from all sin."

We speak, and Christ spoke, of "Solomon in all his glory." Was Solomon finally a penitent and a redeemed man? I like to think that the man who made two great prayers, the prayer when he asked for wisdom and righteousness at the beginning of his reign, and the prayer at the dedication of the temple, was in the end a redeemed man. Certainly none asked for in nobler terms, or understood better, the forgiveness and mercy of God.

Nathan the prophet, the noble tutor of his youth and the friend of his father, said, before Solomon was born, that he would build a house for the glory of God, and if he committed iniquity God would punish him with the rod of men. Then comes this sentence, like the sun breaking out of the western sky at the close of a dark and stormy day: "But my mercy shall not depart away from him." Let every wandering soul remember that! Let everyone who has turned away from the noble dreams and aspirations of his youth remember that!

On the grave of Solomon are two epitaphs. The first can be easily read: "His wives turned away his heart after other gods." But if you bend lower and push back the grass and the weeds, you can read there a second inscription, a second epitaph. It is this, and let us never forget it, for we shall all need it: "My mercy shall not depart away from him."

II

ISAAC—THE MAN WHO DUG OLD WELLS

> "And Isaac digged again the wells of
> water, which they had digged in the days
> of Abraham his father."
>
> GEN. 26:18

ONCE ON A SUMMER DAY, FLOATING DOWN THE OHIO
River, our boat grounded on the sands of a large and
densely wooded island, the largest island in the Ohio,
some distance below Parkersburg. Disembarking, we
roamed over the island and soon came upon the evidences
of a former habitation; fragments of well-cut stones that
had once marked the line of a driveway, and here and
there the vestiges of a once splendid mansion, foundation
stones, broken arches, and fragments of a wall. It was
the home the expatriated Irishman Harman Blennerhassett had built for himself and his lady in that island
wilderness. Once the hospitality of kings was dealt out
there with a lavish hand, and the parks and lawns re-
sounded with European music and cultivated conversation.
The wilderness paradise began to wither when Aaron
Burr entered it and enticed Blennerhassett to join him in
his mysterious enterprise in the Southwest. Now the island
is a river solitude, with only these scattered ruins to speak
of the once lordly home that graced the wilderness.
Wandering about we came upon an old well that had been
dug more than a century before. Someone had rigged a
windlass over it, and we lowered the bucket to a great
depth, raised it again and drank eagerly of the pure and

refreshing water, just as cool and just as refreshing as when Aaron Burr and Blennerhassett and his lovely lady drank of it a century ago. The good water is still there.

That was what Isaac did. He dug again the wells which his father Abraham had dug before him, knowing that he could not improve upon the location of those wells or the water which flowed in their depths.

So far as fame is concerned, Isaac had the misfortune to come between two of the greatest and most striking personalities of the Bible, Abraham, who was his father, and Jacob, who was his son. Isaac was not an innovator. There is nothing striking or dramatic or thrilling in his life, with the exception of his father, Abraham, offering him up on Mount Moriah, and, at the end of his life, his being cheated and deceived by the crafty Jacob, who passed himself off as Esau. Yet Isaac carried on the great tradition of faith in God, and was a necessary link in the chain of the divine purpose and destiny. Some men are great in what they initiate and discover; others are great in what they preserve or rediscover. The last was pre-eminently true of Isaac. We have this set forth in his history, where we are told that he "digged again the wells of water, which they had digged in the days of Abraham his father." The Philistines had filled up the wells that his father Abraham had dug; but Isaac dug them again. He knew that he could not improve on the location of those wells, or on the water which flowed in their depths.

OUR DEBT TO THOSE WHO HAVE GONE BEFORE US

We all owe a debt of gratitude to those who have dug the wells out of which we drink, and planted the trees in whose shade we delight, or whose fruit we eat, and built the bridges over which we cross the chasms and the rivers. When Abraham dug that well he dug it not only for himself, but for Isaac and his generation, and Jacob and his generation, and for the generations to come. "Other men labored, and ye are entered into their labors."

Even in the comforts of life we are indebted to others. How few of the things we enjoy and depend upon we discovered and worked out for ourselves. That match that you strike, the button that you push and which illuminates your house, the car which you start and which conveys you to your work or to another city, the conveniences of home or kitchen, all these someone worked out and discovered for you in the past.

To build for the future, to dig wells for the generations to come, is a mark of greatness. Civilization dies when we think only of today and not of the tomorrows after we are gone. Driving in the country, have you ever seen a row of gracious elm trees, or maples, or poplars, or pines, lining some roadway or driveway leading up to a farmhouse, and thought of the one who planted them? Today those trees give shade and delight and beauty long after the hands that planted them have moldered to dust in the country churchyard, where the shadows of the leaves play to and fro like the shadow of a man's life, or in the little private cemetery on the hilltop, with the picket fence around it. He planted trees for the generation to come.

Traveling once through Scotland on a gloomy wet day, I looked out of the window at a station where the train stopped and saw there the name of the town. It was Auldgarth. The name made me think of the bridge that was built there over the Auldgarth by the father of

[22]

Thomas Carlyle. To that builder and to that bridge Thomas Carlyle paid this tribute in his reminiscences of his father:

A noble craft it is that of the mason. A good building will last longer than most books, than one book in a million. The Auldgarth bridge still spans the water, silently defies its chafing. There hangs it, and will hang, grim and strong, when of all the cunning hands that piled it together, perhaps the last is now powerless in the sleep of death. O Time! O Time! Wondrous and fearful art thou! Yet there is in man what is above thee.

Those who founded and built the United States were thinking not only of themselves but of the generations to come. It was that which animated the godly founders of New England and Pennsylvania. They were zealous to establish and build up a community, an estate, where Christian liberty and Christian principles should prevail. Whenever you pass a college you ought to uncover to those who founded it, thinking not only of themselves and their children but of the generations to come. On the Johnston Memorial Gate of Harvard University you can read inscribed there the words of the Calvinists and the Presbyterians who founded that university:

After God had carried us safe to *New-England,* and we had builded our houses, provided necessaries for our liveli-hood, rear'd convenient places for God's worship and settled the Civill Government; One of the next things we longed for, and looked after was to advance *learning* and perpetuate it to Posterity; dreading to leave an Illiterate Ministry to the Churches, when our present Ministers shall lie in the Dust.

[23]

OLD WELLS NEED TO BE REDUG

The wells that Abraham had dug had to be redug by Isaac before he and his people, his flocks and his herds, could make use of them, for the Philistines had maliciously filled up the wells with sand and rubbish. Isaac did not attempt to dig new wells, for he knew that he could not improve upon the locations that Abraham had selected. What he did was to redig those wells, clear out the rocks and the rubbish and the sand, put new coping around the well, and a new windlass and a rope with which to draw up the water. It was hard work, probably harder than digging the wells in the first place; but he dug them again, and called their names after the names by which his father had called them.

It is folly to think that the only good thing in the world is something that happened before we were born. But it is worse folly to discard useful practices and customs of the past which have proved their merit by time and experience, and upon which God has set the seal of his approval. There are a number of wells which our fathers dug before us, and which need to be redug in our day and generation.

THE WELL OF THE SABBATH

One of these is the well of the Lord's Day. God knew what was good for man when, at the very beginning, he ordained one day out of seven as the day of rest. And now our one day out of seven, the Christian Sabbath, is hallowed by the great memories of Christ and his resurrection. This is the day that lets in the breath and the music of the other world. It gives one a little opportunity to be alone, to face oneself, to salute ourselves and see what our soul doth wear. George Herbert put it well when he said,

> Without thy torch the week were dark;
> Thy torch doth light the way.

An old author, speaking of the journey of life, has quaintly described Sunday as an inn where the traveler rests for a while and collects his thoughts, both of the road he has traveled, and of the destination whither it is leading him. Said Daniel Webster:

You might as well put out the sun, and think to lighten the world with tapers, destroy the attraction of gravity, and think to wield the universe by human powers, as to extinguish the moral illumination of the Sabbath and break this glorious mainspring of the moral government of God.

Both as a public and national institution, and as a personal and spiritual institution, the Sabbath needs to be redug. General Henri Giraud, in his analysis of the fall of France, said that one reason was the negation of everything spiritual, of everything divine, and that atheism, if not proclaimed, was at least encouraged. He said too that part of the spiritual and moral breakdown of France was due to the disregard of the centuries-old practice of observing Sunday as the day of rest. As individuals we would all do well to mark and make this day in our lives different from other days, as Robinson Crusoe did on his lonely isle, when, on the post in front of his stockade, made in the form of a cross, he cut every day a notch with his knife to keep track of the passage of time, and made every seventh notch twice as long as the rest.

[25]

THE WELL OF THE CHRISTIAN HOME

Another well which needs redigging is the well of religion in the home. The old Roman home was never complete and furnished until it had set up the Lares and Penates, the household gods. There are two things that Abraham did wherever he went: one was to dig a well. That was necessary for the physical life of his family and tribe. The other was to build an altar. That was necessary for their spiritual life. The influence of a real Christian home in any community, or in any church, is incalculable. Who can measure the reach and power of the godly home, where daily prayers are offered at the family altar for the members of the household, for loved ones at a distance, for the community in which they dwell, for the government, for the whole family of mankind, and for the coming of Christ's Kingdom? We do not often hear good things out of Hollywood; but recently Cecil DeMille spoke of the profound influence that family prayers had in the life of his boyhood home, and how he himself continues the custom in his own home, and that if it were to be omitted the children would miss it and want to know the reason why. The world and the church, and you and I, need prayer more than we need anything else. And who can measure the influence of prayers going up to God every day from thousands of homes all over our broad land? There is only one kind of a home which can compete with time and grapple with eternity, and that is a Christian home. A young man who had taken service with a well-to-do farmer, after a few weeks gave up his position. A friend asked him why he had left such a good place. Was the work too hard? Or the hours too long? No: he had nothing to complain of on that score. Were the wages too low? No: the wages were generous.

"Why then did you leave?"

"I left," said the man, "because the house had no roof."

That is the significant Scottish expression for a home without prayer to hallow and establish it. "No roof!"

THE WELL OF GOSPEL PREACHING

Another well that needs to be redug is the well of gospel preaching. This is a well which has refreshed many a thirsty soul and many a thirsty generation. But now in many places that well of gospel preaching has been choked up with secularities, with doubts, with concerts, with political discussions, with book reviews. A considerable portion of the preaching of the day would never be recognized by the early apostles as a Christian message, were they to come back and sit in the pew. Without the great tidings of divine love, of atonement, of regeneration, of salvation and the heavenly life to come, preaching is just a discussion, or a lecture, or an entertainment. As Senator Beveridge, the brilliant senator from Indiana, who died some years ago, author of the life of Chief Justice Marshall, and of a life, unfortunately unfinished, of Lincoln, said, when commenting on the true gospel preaching of T. DeWitt Talmage, on whose preaching he frequently waited with profit and delight:

The American people are tired of hearing learned and entertaining lectures delivered under the guise of sermons. They hunger and thirst for the preaching of the faith, unweakened by doubts, criticisms, or explanations, uncompromisingly delivered as Dr. Talmage gave it.

What an immense advantage for the cause of the

Church it would be, if, in all the pulpits of the land, there should ring out in clear and uncompromising accents the great truths of the everlasting gospel—God, the soul, sin, divine love, atonement, forgiveness, salvation, and the everlasting life. Then indeed, as the prophet put it, "With joy shall ye draw water out of the wells of salvation."

THE WELLS OF OUR OWN LIVES
NEED TO BE REDUG

The Philistines are still abroad. They do all they can to fill up and choke the wells of our spiritual life and power. How fares your own well? Does it need redigging? What has choked it and filled it up, so that no longer with joy you draw water out of that well? Is it the neglect of the Bible, of prayer, of meditation, of worship, of Christian work and witness? If so, dig again your well; for there is no substitute for these things.

Traveling one summer to California on one of the great transcontinental trains, I fell to thinking about the first trips I had taken on a train when a lad with my brother and my father. Compared with the standards of today it certainly was a primitive train. The aisles were bare and the seats hard. At the end of the car was the coal stove and the water cooler. From the ceiling of the car hung oil lamps. When the conductor went around to collect the tickets, after he had punched the ticket, he would put the blue or red pasteboard in the hatbands of the male passengers. The engine had a strange-looking smokestack that went out and then in, and then up again, and the pilot, or cowcatcher, not infrequently picked up a real cow. But the thing that I remember most vividly about those early trains was the long box, faced with glass,

[28]

fastened near the door in the front of the car. Under the glass in that box were an ax, with a red handle, a saw, a sledgehammer, and a crowbar; and underneath were the directions to break the glass in case of an emergency. Compared with the modern train that first train seemed primitive indeed. Compared with the massive Diesel engine that was pulling the train over the plains and mountains, the engine of that early train looked like the Christmas toy of a child. This transcontinental train was streamlined and air-cooled and electrically lighted. Its luxuriously fitted cars were walled with aluminum. The dining car was furnished in the style of the best appointed hotels. There were writing rooms and reading rooms and nurses—all the conveniences of city life, as the train rushed on through the day and through the night. But looking out into the corridor from my bedroom, what do you think it was upon which my eye fell? A long box covered with glass, and in the box an ax, a saw, a sledge-hammer, and a crowbar! The very same things that I had seen near the door on my first trip on a train! The intervening years had witnessed a complete transformation in locomotion and in equipment; and yet, for use in emergency, in case of a wreck, there still was the ax and the saw and the sledgehammer and the crowbar. In spite of all the improvements and devices and gadgets of the modern train, if a wreck came and you had to try to hack and hew and saw and hammer your way out, or rescue someone else, you still had to depend upon the ax, the saw, the sledgehammer, and the crowbar! So it is in the great things of the soul, and in the cultivation of the Christian life. The world changes; but there is no improvement over prayer, and the Bible, and worship, and Christian witness and work for the sake of Christ. If those old tools and weapons have become rusty, get them out and polish them up again. If those old wells have become choked, dig them again, as Isaac dug again the wells of water that his father Abraham had dug before him.

When Abraham dug those wells he dug them not only for himself and for his generation, but for Isaac and for his generation, and for the generations to come. I have no doubt that even today, there in the Holy Land, there are men who are still drinking out of one of those wells that Abraham dug, and which Isaac dug again after him. When you dig a well of real Christian character, of spiritual life and power, you bless not only your own life but the lives of others. That must have been what Jesus meant when in the last day of the feast he called men to come unto him and drink, and then said: "He that believeth on me, . . . out of his belly shall flow rivers of living water." That must have been what he meant too, when he said to the woman of Samaria that the water which he was able to give to men would become in them "a well of water springing up into eternal life." That beautiful ministry is possible for every soul who is faithful to Jesus Christ, and is dominated by his spirit. Hundreds can think now of those long since vanished, and who being dead yet speak, because their life and their character were a well of living water unto others. That is the way to live, the way to pray, the way to dig, the way to struggle, the way to aspire, the way to die, so that you may be unto others a well of water in the thirsty stretches of this world. So

> may I reach
> That purest heaven, be to other souls
> That cup of strength in some great agony,

[30]

Enkindle generous ardor, feed pure love,
Beget the smiles that have no cruelty,
Be the sweet presence of a good diffused,
And in diffusion even more intense.
So shall I join the choir invisible
Whose music is the gladness of the world.

III

ACHAN—HOW SIN LOST A BATTLE

> "Behold, they are hid in the earth in
> the midst of my tent, and the silver under
> it."
>
> JOSH. 7:21

THE ONLY TROUBLE WAS THAT HE HAD NOT DUG THE
hole deep enough. That is always the trouble with sin—
you cannot dig a hole deep enough to hide it.

Midnight over the ruins of Jericho. No death-dealing,
blockbuster had fallen on the city. No artillery had blasted
its walls. Yet there it lay, a heap of desolation and ruin.
The moon looks down upon the fragments of gigantic
walls, prostrate pillars of the temples of Baal, the dust
and rubble of baths, theaters, shops, mansions of the rich,
and cottages of the poor.

For seven successive days the army of Joshua had
marched around the walls of Jericho, carrying with them
the Ark of the Covenant, and the priests blowing on the
rams' horns. On the seventh day the army marched
seven times around the walls of the city. When the
seventh circle was completed the people gave a great
shout, and the immense walls of the city fell flat, burying
in their collapse the shops and temples and bazaars and
homes of the people. Of all the inhabitants only one
survived the catastrophe. That one was Rahab the harlot,
who had hid the spies of Israel from their enemies. When
the army of Joshua marched into the fallen city, Rahab

was spared, for, in obedience to the instructions of the spies, she had hung the scarlet thread from her window.

Outside the broken walls of the city the army of Israel lies encamped. The tents of each tribe are pitched around the tribal standard, and in the midst of the camp are the Ark of the Covenant and the tabernacle. In the ruins of Jericho not a soul is alive. In the camp of Israel no one is stirring. All are asleep, all but one. Look! Out of yonder tent comes a solitary man. He stands for a little at the fly of his tent and looks this way and that way to see if anyone is looking. Then, cautiously and carefully, stopping every now and then to look back and make sure that he is unobserved, he makes his way out of the camp of Israel and enters the ruins of Jericho.

There he crouches for a time behind the fragment of a fallen wall, as if fearful of the shadow which his body casts in the moonlight. Now he steps over a column of the temple of Baal and carefully makes his way over the heaps of debris until he reaches the street where the shops had once flourished. There he begins to search amid the ruins. In the moonlight he sees something bright and white shining before him. Reaching down, he finds that it is two hundred shekels of silver. He fills both hands with the silver, and then, opening his fingers, lets the silver flow through his hands like a stream. Once, twice, thrice, he does that, and the sound of the silver falling on silver is music to his covetous soul.

A little farther along he comes upon a wedge of purest gold. Still farther he sees something flashing like fire on the ground. Reaching down he lays hold of the precious stone and finds that it is an ornament on a goodly Babylonian garment. "Better luck than I had expected," he says to himself as he fills his soldier's haversack with the silver, the gold, and the Babylonian garment. Now he cautiously retraces his steps and, leaving the silent and ruined city behind him, enters again the camp of Israel. When he reaches his own tent he pauses and hesitates for a moment, and listens to hear if anyone is stirring in the camp. No one is awake. In the tents of his family all are sound asleep. Then, entering his own tent, and taking the spade that every Israelite carried with him on the march, he digs a hole in the ground at the back of the tent. Into this hole he deposits, first, the Babylonian garment, then the wedge of gold, and then the silver. With his spade he shovels the earth back into the hole, smooths it over, unrolls his mattress over the spot, and lies down to sleep, congratulating himself on the secrecy and great success of his nocturnal expedition. He had brought back with him two hundred shekels of silver, a wedge of gold, and a lordly Babylonian garment, and no eye had seen him! No; no eye but one—the all-seeing eye of God.

Early the next morning, as the mists are lifting on the river Jordan and the Dead Sea to the south, the trumpets begin to speak in the camp of Israel. Three thousand picked soldiers, chosen from all the tribes, obey the voice of the trumpets and, falling in line, march out against the stronghold of Ai, the next fortress in the path of Israel. After the easy victory over mighty Jericho, the capture of Ai was a foregone conclusion. But in the battle which followed, Israel was defeated. Some of the three thousand men were slain, the rest, turning their backs on the enemy, fled in terror to the camp.

Joshua was greatly shaken. It was not the mere repulse before the walls of Ai, in itself an insignificant matter, but that the army of Israel had fled before the heathen. In his distress Joshua fell on his face before God, and

[34]

with him the elders of Israel, with dust on their heads. "Why," asked Joshua of God, "have you brought the people over the Jordan, to deliver them into the hands of the Amorites? It would have been better if they had remained on the other side of Jordan." He feared that the Canaanites and all the inhabitants of the land, hearing of the defeat at Ai, would gather their armies to annihilate the people of Israel.

To this prayer and complaint of Joshua God made a quick answer. He said, "Get thee up; wherefore liest thou thus upon thy face?" This is one of those times when God told a man to stop praying. At the passage of the Red Sea he told Moses to stop praying, and to speak unto the children of Israel that they should go forward. Here he tells Joshua to cease from his complaints and supplications and go into action. He said to Joshua: "Israel hath sinned, and they have also transgressed my covenant which I commanded them; for they have even taken of the accursed thing, and have also stolen, and dissembled also, and they have put it even among their own stuff. Therefore the children of Israel could not stand before their enemies, but turned their backs before their enemies because they were accursed: neither will I be with you any more, except ye destroy the accursed from among you."

At the fall of Jericho the command was given the people that no one was to take of the accursed thing of the spoil of the city, but that all the silver and gold and vessels of brass and iron were to be brought into the treasury of the Lord and consecrated unto the Lord. It was this commandment that some soldier from the camp of Judah had broken on his nocturnal entry into the city. The next morning, in obedience to God, Joshua

[35]

assembled the army and the whole people of Israel, and told them that the reason for their defeat before the walls of Ai was that one of their number had sinned against God by taking of the "accursed thing." To discover who this was, the lot was cast for each tribe and family and household. Reuben, Simeon, Levi, Issachar, Gad, Asher, Benjamin, and all the other tribes passed by and submitted to the lot. But all of them were found innocent. Then came the tribe of Judah. In it family after family was found innocent; household after household; until the lot fell upon Achan. Here was the guilty man!

Joshua called Achan forth before the people and said to him, "My son, give, I pray thee, glory to the Lord God of Israel, and make confession unto him; and tell me now what thou hast done; hide it not from me." Achan then made full confession of his sin, saying, "I have sinned against the Lord God of Israel." He told Joshua how he had seen among the spoils the Babylonish garment, the shekels of silver, and the wedge of gold; how he coveted them and took them, and hid them in the earth in the midst of his tent.

To verify the confession Joshua sent messengers to search his tent, and there, as Achan had told him, they found the silver and the gold and the garment. Bringing them out they laid them on the ground before the people. In solemn procession Joshua then led Achan and his family, with his livestock, his tent, and the stolen and "accursed thing" into the valley of Achor. There he said to Achan, "Why hast thou troubled us? The Lord shall trouble thee this day." And all Israel stoned him with stones. Then they raised over him a great heap of stones, to be a perpetual remembrance of his transgression and of the judgment of God that fell upon him.

This dramatic story from the Book of Joshua tells us several timeless truths about sin: First, how sin gets its start, the progress of sin in the heart, and what it leads to, and how the end of it is death. Second, how sin finds the sinner out; and third, how one man's secret sin affects others and hinders the cause of God in the world.

THE BEGINNING AND PROGRESS OF SIN

In the confession that he made to Joshua, Achan gave the true history of the beginning and progress of sin. What he said was this: "I saw among the spoils a goodly Babylonish garment, and two hundred shekels of silver, and a wedge of gold, . . . then I coveted them, and took them; and, behold, they are hid in the earth in the midst of my tent." First he *saw,* then he *coveted,* then he *took,* then he *hid,* then he *suffered.* That is the natural history of sin. The man and woman, at the very beginning of the world's history, saw that the fruit of the tree was pleasant to the eyes and good for food and desired to make one wise, and they coveted it, and took, and ate, and then sought in vain to hide themselves from God amid the trees of the Garden. Ahab, driving one evening in his chariot to Jezreel, saw the pleasant, well-kept vineyard of Naboth, and coveted it, and took it, after he had slain Naboth. And one day, in that very spot, as Elijah warned him, "where dogs licked the blood of Naboth," there the dogs licked the blood of Ahab. Samson went down to Sorek and saw a beautiful woman, Delilah, and he coveted, and took, and so betrayed his strength to the Philistines, who put out his eyes and made him grind like a beast in the mill. Gehazi, the servant of Elisha, saw the glitter of the gold and silver, and the rich raiment that Naaman the leper had brought from Syria as a gift for the prophet when he healed him, but which Elisha had refused; and he saw, and coveted, and took, and hid in his tent, like Achan, and lied, and went out from the presence of Elisha a leper as white as snow. Judas saw the glitter of the silver in the hands of the priests and Pharisees, and sold his Lord for thirty pieces of silver, and then went out and hanged himself. That is always the natural progress and history of sin. So James put it long ago: "Every man is tempted, when he is drawn away of his own lust, and enticed. Then when lust hath conceived, it bringeth forth sin: and sin, when it is finished, bringeth forth death." The time to resist sin is when it first displays itself and flashes its false attractiveness before us. If it is not resisted then, the next step is to covet, and then to take, and then to seek in vain to hide what has been done.

HOW SIN FINDS THE SINNER OUT

The sin of Achan had all the appearance of a perfect sin, a perfect crime, so far as discovery or apprehension was concerned. It was done in the dead of the night. In the ruins of Jericho there was none who could see, for all were dead. In the camp of Jericho all were asleep. The man who had worn the costly Babylonish garment was dead. The hands that had handled the wedge of gold were forever still. The man who had owned the silver was dead. None of the owners of these things saw the theft. In the camp of Israel, when Achan hid the spoil beneath the ground in his tent, there was none who saw him. None of the camp of the Tribe of Judah, none of the family of Zarah, or the house of Zabdi, to which he belonged. The members of his own family had not stirred when he dug the hole and put the loot into it. When he had smoothed over the ground where it was hid, the ground looked just like the ground everywhere else. Yes, it was a perfect crime. And yet his sin found him out, exposed him, judged him, punished him.

Sin always finds the sinner out: in time, in conscience, in eternity. It finds him out in time. The constitution of the world is moral, and all nature seems to be attuned to the moral law. The proverbs of the nations attest to the universal belief that even in this world sin finds men out in exposure and punishment. When Moses saw an Egyptian smiting a Hebrew, he "looked this way and that way, and when he saw that there was no man, he slew the Egyptian, and hid him in the sand." But the next day, when he saw two Israelites fighting with one another, and sought to separate them, one of them said to him: "Intendest thou to kill me, as thou killedst the Egyptian? And Moses feared, and said, Surely this thing is known." Yes, there is always someone who is looking.

John Donne, onetime secretary and diplomat, gifted poet, and at length a celebrated preacher and dean of St. Paul's, had his first living at Keyston. Walking one day into the churchyard he saw the sexton digging a grave. At length he threw up a skull with his spade. Donne picked it up in his hands and examined it. In the skull, sticking in the temple, he saw a headless nail, which he secretly drew out, and wrapped in the corner of his handkerchief. Then he asked the gravedigger if he knew whose skull it was. The gravedigger said he did. It had been a man's who kept a rum shop, a drunken, dissipated fellow who one morning was found dead in bed after he had taken two quarts of liquor the night before. "Had he a wife?" Donne asked.

"Yes."

"Is she living?"

"Yes."

"What character does she bear?"

"A very good one; only her neighbors reflect on her because she married the day after her husband was buried."

Sometime afterwards, in the course of his pastoral visits, Donne called on this woman. He asked her a number of questions, among others, what sickness her husband died of. She told him about his having taken the two quarts of liquor and how he was found dead in bed the next morning. Whereupon Donne opened his handkerchief and, holding up the nail before the woman, said, "Woman, do you know this nail?" The woman instantly acknowledged the crime, and in due season was punished for it.

Sin finds men out in conscience. After all others have lost the trail of an evil deed, and given up the search for the evil doer, conscience takes up its own inexorable search and inflicts its own inescapable judgment.

If it were done when 'tis done!

But that is just the trouble with sin—it is never done. The reaction of conscience may be immediate, as in the case of Judas, when he flung down the blood money before the priests and said, "I have sinned." As in the case of Peter, who, when Jesus looked upon him after he had denied him that night in the court of Caiaphas, went out and wept bitterly. But sometimes the reaction and punishment of conscience may be long deferred, as it was in the case of the brethren of Joseph, when long years after they had sold him as a slave into Egypt, and they had come down to buy corn in Egypt, and Joseph demanded that one of them be left as a hostage until they brought down their youngest brother, the conscience-smitten men said to one another: "We are verily guilty concerning our brother, in that we saw the anguish of his soul, when he besought us, and we would not hear; therefore is this distress come upon us." Conscience may sleep in prosperity, only to awaken in the storm of adversity.

> Though no mortal ere accused you
> Though no witness ere confused you,
> Though the darkness came and fell;
> Over even deeds of hell.

> Still your secret sin will find you
> Pass before your eyes to blind you,
> Burn your heart with hidden shame,
> Scar your cheek with guilty flame.

HOW SIN HURTS AND HINDERS OTHERS

Sin is always individual in its origin, but always social, as well as individual, in its results. No man liveth unto himself, and no man sinneth unto himself. Here was a secret sin if ever there was one. None of all the army and camp of Israel had seen it, and yet its effect upon Israel was disastrous. When they went out to battle against Ai they fled before the enemy. And the reason, God told Joshua, was because of the sin of one man. That sin brought defeat to his country on the field of battle. It brought disgrace and ruin to his family. It brought doom and ruin to himself.

Who can tell how much the work and battle of the church is held up and hindered because of Achans in the camp? How solemn that makes the responsibility of every soldier in the ranks of the army of the Lord, of every professed follower of Christ in the church! To whatever degree you are unworthy or un-Christlike in spirit, in word, or in deed, to that extent you hinder the work of the church and hold up the progress of the army of the Lord.

Not only does a single sin, even the most secret sin, affect and influence other lives, but it goes on, year after year, sometimes age after age, doing its malignant work. That is the meaning of that monotonous refrain that you hear echoing in the Old Testament, "Jeroboam the son of Nebat, who made Israel to sin." Long after Jeroboam was dead, the sin which he had committed, when he put up his golden calves for idols, and so led Israel into idolatry, haunted and injured the nation.

A man once went into a jewelry shop in Paris to purchase a ring. The jeweler brought out a tray of rings for him to inspect and from which to make his selection. As he was looking them over, he showed him, as a curiosity, a medieval ring of the finest gold and workmanship, and so fabricated that on the inside of the band there was a tiny claw of a lion, but so cut that it did not irritate the finger when the ring was first put on. The man slipped the ring on his finger, made some comment about it, and then handed it back to the jeweler. When he had purchased a ring for himself he returned to his home. That night he felt a numbness in his hand, and then in his arm, and at length his whole side seemed to be paralyzed. A physician was summoned, and, after examining the man, said to him that he had all the symptoms of poisoning. But the man could think of no way in which he had been poisoned. Then the physician discovered a slight scratch on the finger of the paralyzed hand, and the man remembered the medieval ring that he had seen that day at the jeweler's and had slipped on his finger. This was one of the rings that the cruel heads of the Italian states of that age made use of when they wished to get rid of an enemy. In the tiny claw of the lion was a duct which was filled with the most deadly poison. The ring would be presented to the victim as a gift. Sometime afterwards the one who had given him the ring would salute him in a friendly fashion, and, taking his hand, would press it in a way that drove the tiny claw of the lion into the skin and thus injected the poison. In a short time the man would die. Thus four hundred years after the ring had been made it still had the power to kill. So is it with sin. That is one of the things which helps us to understand why it is that nothing less than the precious blood of Christ can atone for sin and wash out its stain.

Great as was the sin of Achan, and tragic its effect and influence upon others, and inescapable though his judgment was, Achan made a full confession of his sin. That is the only compensation that the sinner can ever render unto God. If anyone has made himself an enemy of his own soul, of his family, of his church, of his community, by his transgression, the one good thing that he can do is to repent and confess his sin. "If we say that we have no sin, we deceive ourselves, and the truth is not in us. If we confess our sins, he is faithful and just to forgive us our sins, and to cleanse us from all unrighteousness." Achan was stoned; but Christ was beaten, crucified on our behalf, that through his death we might have life eternal.

IV

BARNABAS—THE GOOD MAN BEHIND A GREAT MAN

"Barnabas, . . . son of consolation."

Acts 4:36

WHEN PAUL AND BARNABAS HEALED THE LAME MAN AT Lystra, the people concluded that they were gods come down to visit the earth, and if the apostles had not restrained them, they would have offered a sacrifice to them. The people called Paul "Mercury," because he was the chief speaker, but they called Barnabas "Jupiter." The superior presence and mien of Barnabas evidently greatly impressed these fickle people of Lystra. In the New Testament narrative Barnabas has a certain noble and majestic way with him.

This is a sermon I found at Antioch, when leaning over the parapet of the bridge and watching the snow-colored Orontes flowing rapidly through the city toward the sea. I found it on the broken rocks of the quay at Selucia, where the world's greatest voyage commenced when Paul and Barnabas set sail for Cyprus. I found it in the market place of Salamis on Cyprus, where they first preached on that island, and where, according to the tradition, Barnabas afterwards suffered martyrdom, being stoned by the enraged populace. I found it when passing through Antioch of Pisidia; and on the broad mountain-guarded plains of Galatia; at Iconium and at Lystra and Derbe; and at Attalia, the lonely harbor on the southern coast of Asia

Minor, whence the apostles sailed on their return journey. Everywhere one goes where Paul went, one thinks of his earliest, and in some respects greatest, companion in the work of the gospel.

There are mountains which, if separated from other and higher mountains, would impress one as lofty peaks; but when seen in the company of Pike's Peak or Mount Everest or Mount McKinley they are not impressive. Barnabas had the misfortune, if you can call it such, of appearing in history by the side of Paul. And who in comparison with that mountainous man will not seem of little stature? But Barnabas, it is well to remember, was not only a good man, but a great man in his own right. Furthermore he played a great and important part in the life of Paul. Humanly speaking, if there had been no Barnabas there would have been no Paul.

Barnabas was not the name given him by his parents. His real name was Joseph; but the apostles and disciples of the Church gave him this surname, Barnabas, which means "son of consolation." They had seen Barnabas encourage and comfort so many people that his real name was lost sight of and he was known everywhere in the church as the comforter, the encourager, and the exhorter. There are some remarkable changes of names recorded in the Bible. God changed Abram's name to Abraham, for he was to be father of a people. After his midnight wrestle with the angel, the name of Jacob, the supplanter, was changed to Israel, the prince with God. Christ himself changed Simon's name to Peter, which means "a rock." Saul of Tarsus, for reasons not altogether clear, became known, not as Saul, but as Paul; and here the disciples, observing the ruling trait in the life of Joseph, began to call him Barnabas, the "son of consolation."

[45]

Barnabas was a native of the Island of Cyprus. He was the owner of land there, which in that day meant that he was a man of means. But when he was converted, perhaps on the Day of Pentecost, in Jerusalem, he sold his lands in Cyprus and put all the money into the treasury of the Church. His Christian life commenced with this act of complete surrender and the renunciation of the things of this world. He soon became known as Barnabas, the "good man, full of the Holy Ghost and of faith." There are a number of occasions upon which Barnabas showed how he deserved the name or title, the "son of consolation," which the Church had given him.

BARNABAS BEFRIENDS PAUL

The first of these occasions was in connection with Paul. After his conversion at Damascus, Paul immediately began to preach in Damascus that the Jesus whom he had persecuted was the Messiah and the Son of God. Driven out of Damascus, barely escaping with his life, Paul made his way to Jerusalem. As he approached the gates of the city we wonder if he had any misgiving. Did he recall the dark chapter of persecution which he had written there: how he had haled men and women to prison, and how he had held the garments of them that stoned Stephen? Did he begin to think that perhaps none of the disciples would listen to him or give him the right hand of fellowship? The probability is that Paul was so full of enthusiasm and zeal for the Christ he had found, or who in so remarkable a way had found him, that he never stopped to think about the welcome he would receive by the Christians at Jerusalem. If, at Damascus, Ananias had come to visit him and had given him the right hand of fellowship, saying to him, "Brother Saul, receive thy sight," surely, Paul must have thought to himself, the Christians at Jerusalem will receive me.

But when Paul appeared at Jerusalem he received a rude awakening. No door was opened to him. The Jews despised him as a renegade. The Christians were all afraid of him and suspicious of him. "Is not this the man," they must have said among themselves, "who persecuted and wasted the Church, dragged our people before the synagogues and into prison? Isn't he the man who held the clothes of the murderers of Stephen? Are his hands not red with blood? His profession of the faith is only a ruse. He intends to worm himself into our confidence, only in order that he may betray us to our enemies. Can this savage wolf suddenly have been transformed into a lamb? Can the blasphemer and the persecutor have become a disciple and a preacher?"

This was what the disciples, we gather from the record, said and felt. Every door was shut against Paul. Peter, James, and even John, would have nothing to do with him. How bitter and trying an hour that was for Paul. What keener anguish can the soul have than to have its sincere professions of faith and piety taken for a pretense and hypocrisy. And yet Paul must have recognized that his record had been such as to merit him such a reception from the Christians at Jerusalem.

It was a crisis in Paul's life. He might have been lost to the Church. I do not believe that Paul could ever have denied his Lord, or forsaken the Christian faith, but he might have been lost to the Church, and the door of great opportunity might never have opened for him had it not been for the noble and magnanimous and sympathetic Barnabas. Barnabas was the only one who gave Paul a welcome. He took him to the apostles, to Peter and James

[47]

and John, and told them what had happened to Paul since he had left Jerusalem, how the Lord had appeared unto him and had spoken words to him, and how he had proved his sincerity by preaching the gospel at the risk of his life at Damascus. You can imagine Barnabas arguing with those pillars of the Church at Jerusalem! "You must," he says, "give Paul a chance. I am convinced of his sincerity. I have listened to his account of his conversion. He is a man of great talent, and if he has a chance will do a great work for Christ here and elsewhere." So urgent and eloquent was Barnabas that he convinced the apostles. James, John, Peter—all took Paul in, and the Christians now regarded him as a fellow disciple. No man ever did a more beautiful piece of work for another, or for the world, than Barnabas did for Saul. If Barnabas had disappeared from the sacred narrative with just this one mention and this one achievement, his name would be immortal.

Barnabas "took" Paul. He took him to the apostles and spoke for him when Paul was down, under suspicion, and when no man would have anything to do with him. It is not hard to take a man and speak for him when he is up, when he is sailing prosperously before the wind, when everyone is praising him; but to take a man when he is down, that is another matter.

After the battle of Shiloh, the first great battle of the Civil War, in which General Grant narrowly escaped defeat and disaster, a storm of criticism and slander came down upon the head of Grant. He was charged with gross carelessness, incompetence, and drunkenness. General Halleck, who commanded the Department of Missouri, joined Grant's army, and thus Grant was reduced to a mere figurehead. His position had become intolerable to him and he determined to resign from the army. As he was packing his boxes one day at his headquarters, Sherman, who had heard of the matter and of his plan to resign, came to see him and pleaded with him to reconsider his resolution. He reminded him that there had been a time when he had felt the way Grant did, but now all was prosperous with him. He was sure it would be so with Grant if he stayed with the army. Some happy event would come along and everything would be changed. Grant, somewhat reluctantly, agreed to stay in the army. In a few weeks the "happy event" which Sherman had foretold came along in the appointment of General Halleck to the command of all the armies at Washington. This put Grant again in the active leadership of his army, and the path was opened for him to Vicksburg, Chattanooga, Missionary Ridge, the Wilderness, and Appomattox.

In thus rescuing Paul and establishing him in the confidence of the early Church, Barnabas showed that fine ability to get within another's mind, to share another's feelings. He understood how Paul must have felt, and did all that he could to lift the cloud of suspicion from the apostle's life. His act on behalf of Paul also showed that Barnabas was worthy of the encomium pronounced upon him, "a good man, full of the Holy Ghost and of faith." He was indeed full of faith, and, in contrast with most of the disciples—perhaps all the disciples at Jerusalem—Barnabas had faith that the Holy Spirit could convert and change even a wicked blasphemer and bloodstained persecutor like Saul of Tarsus.

BARNABAS SPEAKS FOR THE GENTILES

The second time that we see Barnabas earning the right to his name "the son of consolation," is at Antioch. In that great and beautiful city on the Orontes there was a large population of people who spoke Greek. From far off Cyrene in North Africa, and from the nearby island of Cyprus, Greek-speaking Jewish Christians began to teach and to preach among the people of Antioch. They met with an immediate response, and large numbers of Greeks began to press into the Church. This preaching is an example of how God makes the wrath of man to praise him. Some of the disciples who were driven out of Jerusalem at the time of the martyrdom of Stephen and the subsequent persecution were men from Cyrene and Cyprus. These were the ones who preached the Word to the people of Antioch.

When the Church at Jerusalem heard about these Gentiles and Greeks coming into the Church there was great excitement. Many shook their heads and said, "This will never do. The gospel is for the lost sheep of the house of Israel, not for the outside world." But Barnabas, recognized as a man of judgment and of great kindness and sympathy, was appointed by the disciples to go down to Antioch and look the situation over. A man of lesser parts and shorter vision might have reported, "There is too much excitement, too much emotion, in this revival. These people only yesterday were serving idols. They ought to pass through a period of trial and probation. It's too much of a mass movement, too many wanting to do the same thing at the same time. I recommend that we do not recognize this movement as genuine, and that these people be not admitted to the Church." But instead of that, this, Luke tells us, is what Barnabas did. "When he came, and had seen the grace of God, [he] was glad, and exhorted them all, that with purpose of heart they would cleave unto the Lord." And the reason for Barnabas' judgment and action, Luke immediately adds: "For he was a good man, and full of the Holy Ghost and of faith."

This was perhaps the greatest crisis in the history of the Christian Church. The gate was opening for the evangelization of the world, for the preaching of the gospel, as Christ had promised, unto the uttermost parts of the earth. What would have happened if a blind and bigoted Church had repudiated the work at Antioch and shut the door against the Gentile Christians? It was a great crisis indeed, and the credit for the solution of it belongs in large part to a good and great man—Barnabas. In a real sense Barnabas was a bridge by which Jerusalem and Judaistic Christianity passed over to a world-wide Kingdom of God.

BARNABAS RESCUES PAUL FROM OBSCURITY

Barnabas for the third time shows his right to his name "son of consolation" in his next meeting with Saul of Tarsus. Although Barnabas had persuaded the Christians at Jerusalem to accept Paul as a disciple, it was impossible for him to preach there because of the persecution of the enraged Jews. In order to save his life they sent Paul down to the coast to Caesarea, where he took a ship for Tarsus.

Paul must have felt disheartened and discouraged. During his long wait in Tarsus, as he went up and down the narrow streets of that ancient city, probably shunned and scorned by his fellow Hebrews, he perhaps said to himself, "Where is the fulfillment of the promise given me that I was to be a chosen vessel to Christ and to bear his name before the Gentiles and kings and the children of Israel?"

Meanwhile, as Paul waited, chafing at inaction and retirement in Tarsus, the work of the Spirit was proceeding at Antioch. Soon Barnabas saw that he could not handle the situation by himself. He must have an associate, someone who was qualified to lead this great work, for "much people was added unto the Lord." Whom could he secure? Barnabas named over some of the leaders of that day— Simeon and Lucius and Mananen. No, none of these would do. What about Peter and James and John? None of these would do either. Then Barnabas said to himself, "Saul of Tarsus! He is the man! He can speak the Greek language. He himself has been brought up in a great Greek city. He knows the approach to the Greek mind. He has the purity of character, the Christian zeal, and the Christian experience."

Barnabas took no chances with a messenger, but went himself to Tarsus, a considerable journey for that day, and searched out Paul. He told him that he had found the right place for him, that a door was opened to him at Antioch, and that a great opportunity awaited him. On the very next ship, no doubt, Paul went back to Seleucia and up to Antioch with Barnabas, and with his magnificent enthusiasm and zeal entered into the work among the Gentiles.

That was a notable service that Barnabas rendered Paul. He brought him out of retirement, led him onto the arena of his life's work. Now, with Paul preaching at Antioch, the grand missionary history of the Church is about to begin. Soon the Holy Spirit will say, "Separate me Barnabas and Saul for the work whereunto I have called them." Paul and Barnabas sail from Antioch to Cyprus on the world's most memorable voyage. Henceforth Barnabas is no longer the leader. He fades, as it were, from the picture, and the chief figure becomes Paul. But wherever you see that grand heroic character on his journeys up and down Asia and into Europe, look carefully, and you will see by his side the shadow of another man, the man who introduced Paul to his life's work, the good man behind the great man—Barnabas, the "son of consolation."

Barnabas may be described as a good man behind a great man. The prophet Samuel was that kind of a man, although he was also as great as he was good. But he is the man who introduces great men chosen of God for the work of his Kingdom. It was Samuel who called and anointed Saul to be king over Israel, although that meant the eclipse of his own leadership and fame, for Israel was now to be ruled by a king, instead of by the aged prophet. When Saul failed and was rejected of God, it was Samuel again who was sent to call and anoint David, the son of Jesse, as king over Israel.

All through history you will find instances of good men, and great men too, who bring great world figures onto the stage of their action. Late on a summer afternoon, in 1536, three travelers, two men and a woman, coming along the road that leads from France to Switzerland, reached the crest of the hills to the west of Geneva, and paused to enjoy the view of that earthly paradise which has enchanted so many thousands of travelers. At their feet lay the beautiful lake, "clear, placid Léman," and on its farther bank the clustering houses of Geneva, surmounted by the towers of St. Peter's church. Past what is now called the Isle of Rousseau, the blue waters of the lake flow out to form the River Rhone. As far as the eye can see, in every direction, mountain ranges pile themselves one upon another.

The three travelers are two brothers and a sister. One of these brothers, the one with the high brow and the

[53]

black pointed beard and the lustrous eyes, although only twenty-seven years of age, is already a famous scholar, and has written one of the world's greatest books. It was only by accident that John Calvin came that evening to Geneva. He was on his way to make his home at Basel, the resort of scholars and thinkers. The wars between France and the Empire had closed the direct route from Noyon to Basel, and he had taken the roundabout route through Geneva. He had intended to rest there for the night only, but a friend who recognized him hurried off to tell William Farel, the leader of the Reformation party at Geneva, that John Calvin was at the village inn. Down to the inn hurried Farel, determined that this young scholar should remain in Geneva and carry on the work of the Reformation. Destiny was made that night in the room at the inn. Calvin protested that his work was that of a scholar, and that he was ill-fitted to lead the battle of the Reformation at Geneva. He had long looked forward to a period of retirement and study at Basel. To this impetuous Farel answered: "You think of nothing but rest. You trouble about nothing else than your studies. Well, then, in the Name of the Almighty, I tell you that unless you give ear to his call, your plans he will not bless! May God curse your rest! Do you hear what I say? May God curse your studies if, in such urgent need, you dare hold back and refuse to give help and support!" Stirred and alarmed at this fearful adjuration, Calvin bowed his head in assent. God had spoken. Thus it was that William Farel introduced Calvin to the work of the Reformation at Geneva, and to the everlasting good of the Church and of mankind.

BARNABAS SAVES MARK

Barnabas and Paul had an unhappy dispute over Mark, who had turned back on the first voyage, and whom Paul refused to take with him the second time. The dispute was so sharp that Paul and Barnabas separated. As far as we know they never met again. That was sad indeed. But let us not waste too many tears over it. There are some people who have not sufficient conviction to get into a controversy over anything. That is no credit to them. But Barnabas and Paul were men of deep conviction. In a sense both were right and both were wrong in this dispute. Paul was right in not wanting to have with him a man who had proved a quitter and a coward, although we may think that he might have stretched a point in view of all that Barnabas had done for him in the past. Yet, although we regret this sad dispute and final separation, it tells us what a man this Apostle Paul was: a man who would unhesitatingly sacrifice the dearest friendship and personal relationship if he thought it stood in the way of his Christian duty. Barnabas was right in that he wished to give Mark another chance. He was able to put himself into the place and into the mind of another man. His confidence in Mark proved to be well grounded, for he restored himself so nobly that even Paul at the end of his life wrote to Timothy to bring Mark with him to be his companion and helper in the last hours at Rome. It is this Mark who was the author of the second Gospel. When you read the pages of that Gospel, if you are familiar with the history of Mark, you will see written across the pages of his Gospel not only the name of Peter, who told Mark the story of Christ's life, but the name of Barnabas, the "son of consolation," without whom Mark would never have written the Gospel.

[55]

BARNABAS SITS FOR PAUL

There, then, is Barnabas, the "son of consolation." He was a man who was ever ready to look on the good and hopeful side. He was a man who was ready to believe the best concerning his brother man, and who had faith in the power of the gospel to change even a wicked persecutor like Saul of Tarsus into the greatest friend and apostle of Christ. He was a man without pride and jealousy. As John said of Jesus, so Barnabas could say of Paul, "He must increase, but I must decrease." He was a man who took delight in discovering pre-eminent qualities in other men, and introducing them to their life's work. He was a man who was ready to speak for his brother man who was under a cloud of suspicion.

Not many are fitted or designed to be Johns or Peters or Pauls, but all of us by the grace of Christ can be what Barnabas was, a "son of consolation," men and women anxious and ready to encourage and strengthen and help others, to be the cup of strength to other souls in the midst of their sorrow, their trials, and their agony.

Paul lived to write a great and beautiful description of a Christian man. He describes that man in the immortal accents of the thirteenth chapter of I Corinthians, as having the love that suffereth long, and is kind; that envieth not; that vaunteth not itself; that seeketh not its own; that rejoiceth not in iniquity, but rejoiceth in the truth; that beareth all things, believeth all things, and hopeth all things.

When I read that beautiful chapter, that masterpiece of Paul's inspired brush, I feel sure that the model, the man that Paul had in mind, was his old friend Barnabas— the "son of consolation."

V

CALEB—A MAN, NOT A GRASSHOPPER

> "He wholly followed the Lord God of
> Israel."
>
> JOSH. 14:14

THAT WAS SAID OF CALEB BY MOSES. IT WAS SAID OF
Caleb by himself also. Most important of all, it was said
of Caleb by God. "My servant Caleb, because he had another spirit with him, and hath followed me fully, him
will I bring into the land whereinto he went." Whenever
God says that of a man, that he has followed him fully,
the man who has such a mark upon him, and such praise
recorded of him, is well worthy of our study and considera-
tion.

Caleb is one of the men in the Bible whom I have always admired. His courage, his promptness, his daring,
and the magnificent spirit of his old age, when he won his
greatest victory, have always stirred me.

On their march out of Egypt the children of Israel had
reached Kadesh on the southern boundary of Canaan.
This was the Land of Promise, toward which they were
marching. But before they entered it, Moses sent twelve
spies, one for each tribe, into the land to make a recon-
naissance and bring back a report concerning its inhabitants, its fertility, its cities, and its fortifications. There
was no doubt in the mind of Moses that, according to the
promise, the people of Israel were to possess this land.
The spies were not sent into it because there was any un-
certainty as to whether they could possess it, but rather to

prepare the people for its conquest. The land was to be theirs. There was no doubt about that. There is no "if" about the promises of God. The only "if" is in man's behavior and obedience or disobedience.

After a forty days' exploration of the land of Canaan the twelve spies returned to the camp of Israel at Kadesh. It must have been a stirring and moving sight when the trumpet sounded in the camp and summoned the people to hear the report of the spies who had returned from Canaan. First the majority, that is, ten out of the twelve, made their report. They said it was a good land, flowing with milk and honey, and a very fruitful and fertile land. As evidence of that they had brought back with them a cluster of grapes so heavy and rich that it required two men to carry it between them over their shoulders on a pole. All of us in our childhood remember seeing the picture of those two men carrying the huge cluster of grapes between them.

So far so good. But that was not all. Now came the other side of the picture, the "nevertheless" of the ten spies. They said that the land was inhabited by fierce tribes, the Amalekites in the south, the Hittites, the Amorites, and the Jebusites in the mountains, and the Canaanites by the sea. These warlike tribes dwelt in strong, high-walled cities; and there too they had seen the sons of Anak, men of gigantic stature, so large, they said, that "we were in our own sight as grasshoppers, and so we were in their sight."

When the people heard this discouraging report, affected and infected by the cowardice and fear of the ten spies, they lifted up their voices and wept, and murmured against Moses and Aaron: "Would God that we had died in the land of Egypt! or would God we had died in this wilderness! . . . Let us make a captain, and let us return into Egypt." Then it was that Caleb stood forth and made the heroic minority report, for himself and for Joshua. "He stilled the people," and said, "Let us go up at once, and possess it, for we are well able to overcome it. . . . Rebel ye not against the Lord, neither fear ye the people of the land; for they are bread for us: their defense is departed from them, and the Lord is with us: fear them not." But the congregation of the people were in no mood to listen to Caleb's heroic exhortation. Instead, they cried out for Caleb and Joshua to be stoned.

The anger of the Lord was kindled against the people for their cowardice and lack of faith. But after the beautiful prayer of that great interceder Moses, who said: "Pardon, I beseech thee, the iniquity of this people according unto the greatness of thy mercy, and as thou hast forgiven this people, from Egypt even until now," God said: "I have pardoned according to thy word: but as truly as I live, all the earth shall be filled with the glory of the Lord."

The people were spared immediate destruction; but because of their unbelief, and their cowardice and disobedience, after having seen the glory of God and his miracles which he did in Egypt and in the wilderness, God said to Moses that none of them, that is, those who were grown men and women, should see the Promised Land. All those from twenty years upward who had listened to the report of the ten spies, and scorned the report of Joshua and Caleb, were to perish in the wilderness. Israel, then arrived at the borders of the Promised Land, for its disobedience was turned back into the wilderness, where the people wandered for forty years, marching to and fro, one year for every day the spies had spent in the exploration of the land of Canaan. When, after forty years, the people came to Kadesh again, the wilderness paths were strewn with the bones of that generation which had refused to enter the Land of Promise.

THE EVIL INFLUENCE OF FALSE AND UNBELIEVING LEADERS

Ten men led the whole people astray. The twelve spies represented each one of the twelve tribes, and were princes, each of them, in their tribe. But ten of them were altogether unworthy of the post of leadership to which Moses had appointed them. It was not only a just punishment on the people that they were sent back into the wilderness to wander for forty years, but a wise measure on the part of God, for the people, led by such cowardly leaders, could not have been used of God to conquer the land of Canaan. These ten infected the whole host with their cowardice. They felt themselves to be grasshoppers in the presence of the giants of Canaan, and it was a natural result, what they themselves stated in their report, "and so we were in their eyes." If you feel yourself to be a grasshopper-man, others will look upon you and treat you as a grasshopper.

If they had had the spirit of courage and faith, Israel might have entered and conquered the land in forty days, instead of waiting for forty years. But because of their unbelief the conquest of the land had to be postponed for forty years. How often it has happened in history that victories of justice and righteousness and humanity have had to be postponed because of unbelief and lack of courage. The memoirs of Winston Churchill make clearer than ever the fact that a certain dread of meeting Germany in arms, and with that a dangerous policy of appeasement, made the terrible and bloody struggle of World War II, with its millions of dead and maimed, and rivers of blood staining the earth, inevitable. When Hitler marched his troops into the Ruhr in 1938, a strong and courageous attitude on the part of France and England could easily have driven him out, and probably averted the bloody struggle which soon followed. The same is no doubt true of the history of slavery in the United States. The constant appeasement of slaveholders and compromises with the South in the end made the struggle all the more desperate and bloody.

This is always true in the warfare of the Church with evil and the kingdom of Satan. Peter has a very significant and arresting phrase, in which, speaking of the coming of Christ with its judgments and its blessings, he says that the disciples of Christ, in all holy conversation and godliness, ought to be "looking for and *hasting* unto the coming of the day of God, wherein the heavens being on fire shall be dissolved, and the elements shall melt with fervent heat. Nevertheless we, according to his promise, look for new heavens and a new earth, wherein dwelleth righteousness." This would seem to suggest that the great day of the Lord may be hastened by faithful praying and courageous Christians. In the original, the phrase which we translate "hasting unto the coming of the day of God" has no "unto" in it, and reads "hasting"—or making sooner—the coming of Christ. According to this, the long postponement of that great day of victory and conquest is due to the lack of faith and belief and witness on the part of the followers of Christ.

Every Christian man is, as it were, a spy who has been sent out to report concerning the land of faith and belief. What kind of a report do you bring? Is it of a nature to discourage other men, as that report of the ten spies discouraged the people of Israel and made them afraid to go up and possess the land? The world is full of evil, and there are giants of iniquity, and the tides of the world run ever against God and the Church. What do you see? Only these giants, or do you see also the powers of the invisible world and the victory of him who doeth his will in the armies of heaven and among the inhabitants of the earth? No Christian should be a man of discouraging and evil report. It was an old provision of the law of Israel that when the army went forth to battle, those who were afraid should be permitted to go back to their homes, lest they should make the hearts of their fellow soldiers to melt with fear. So it was that Gideon's army of 32,000 was reduced by the first test of fear to 10,000, and yet the army was stronger with the 22,000 cowards out of it than it was with them in it.

What kind of a report do you bring? What does your life, your joy, your spirit, say about the Christian life and the kingdom of heaven? Can you tell others that the "gold of that land is good"?

CALEB AND THE MINORITY REPORT

Caleb too and Joshua caught a glimpse of the fierce Amalekites and Amorites and Jebusites and Hittites who held the land of Canaan. They too saw the formidable walls and fortifications, and they too were amazed at the stature of the giants. And yet their report differed altogether from the report of the ten. They said: "Let us go up at once and possess it, . . . for they are bread for us. . . . The Lord is with us: fear them not."

Caleb remembered the mighty deeds and miracles that God had wrought in the past for Israel: how he had opened a way for them through the Red Sea, had brought water

[62]

for them out of the rock, had conquered all enemies in their path, and had led them with the pillar of cloud by day and the pillar of fire by night. They believed too the great promises and assurances which God had given them that they could possess the land. "Let us go up; . . . the Lord is with us." Because Caleb believed in God he was not afraid of the giants. He was no grasshopper in his own sight; neither would he have been a grasshopper in the sight of those giants, had the long-postponed battle with the giants come off at that time.

This was the courage born of trust and faith. Caleb believed in God and was not afraid of giants. The Church of Christ today, as it faces the world, needs that "other spirit" of Caleb. Gigantic evils confront it: unbelief, atheism, sensuality, licentiousness, in every branch of life; political despotism and tyranny, godless communism. But is that all the Christian is permitted to see? Is there no other host upon which he can look? Is it only these giants of iniquity that he beholds, and not the mighty captain of our salvation? Let us remember what the Church of the living God is. It is the pillar and ground of the truth. It is the Church which Christ loved. It is the Church which he purchased with his own precious blood. It is the Church which has salted and blessed mankind in past ages. It is the Church of which Christ said, "The gates of hell shall not prevail against it." It is the Church to which he has promised a day of glorious victory, when the kingdoms of this world shall become the kingdoms of our Lord and of his Christ; when Christ shall put every enemy under his feet and God shall be all and in all; a day when Christ shall receive the heathen for his inheritance and the uttermost parts of the earth for a possession; a day so glorious that, compared with it, the brightest day that has yet

[63]

dawned upon the world is midnight, and the fairest splendors which have invested it but the shadow of darkness.

You remember the story of Elisha when he was surrounded by the Assyrian host at Dothan. The servant of Elisha, Gehazi, no doubt, rose up early in the morning and walked on the top of the walls of the city. The rising sun was reflected upon the chariots, the helmets, the shields and spears of the great army of Syria which completely surrounded the city. In dismay Gehazi left the wall of the city and, running down to Elisha, his master, said, "Alas, my master! how shall we do?" But Elisha said to him, "Fear not: for they that be with us are more than they that be with them." And Elisha prayed, and said, "Lord, I pray thee, open his eyes, that he may see. And the Lord opened the eyes of the young man; and he saw: and, behold, the mountain was full of horses and chariots of fire round about Elisha." That is the vision the Church of Christ needs today. Formidable as evil appears to be, in reality it is always weak and always conquerable. The tribesmen of Canaan were fierce and the giants were mighty. But if Israel had had the spirit of Caleb and Joshua, they could have conquered the land in forty days.

CALEB FOLLOWED THE LORD WHOLLY

The secret of Caleb's strength and courage and faith was that "he wholly followed the Lord." There are few in the Bible of whom that could be said. And what is the situation today? The situation is that the vast number of us who are in the Church are quite satisfied to follow the Lord now and then, partly, occasionally, but not "fully," not "wholly," as Caleb did. The mighty influence of the great men of God was due to the fact that they followed the Lord "wholly," not partly. That was what Paul said: "This one thing I do, forgetting those things which are behind, . . . I press toward the mark for the prize of the high calling of God in Christ Jesus."

In his second visit to Europe, in 1872, Dwight L. Moody, at an early morning meeting in a haymow near Dublin, heard Henry Varley say in a quiet way: "The world has yet to see what God can do with and for and through and in a man who is fully and wholly consecrated to him." The next Sabbath, sitting high up in Spurgeon's tabernacle in London, in the same seat he had occupied in 1867, Moody, as he thrilled to the preaching of Spurgeon, was hearing over and over again those words of Varley. He said to himself, "The world has yet to see! With and for and through and in a man! Varley meant any man! Varley didn't say he had to be educated, or brilliant, or anything else—just a man! Well, by the Holy Spirit in me, I will be one of those men!" Sympathetic Christians who went to talk with him, thinking that he was under the conviction of sin, learned that it was not a case of sin or penitence, but great joy, the joy of dedication to a high purpose. Henceforth it was a life like that of Caleb. Moody followed "wholly" the Lord his God.

CALEB'S VICTORY IN HIS OLD AGE

The great victory of Caleb, and the great reward, came when he was an aged man. Through all those forty years of wandering in the wilderness he never lost his faith in God, and never forgot the promise that God had made to him and Joshua: that although all their contemporaries should whiten the wilderness with their bones for their unbelief, they two, of all the host, should enter into Canaan and possess the land. What a long wait that was for Caleb! He saw his contemporary generation perish one by one.

He saw Moses and Aaron disappear as the leaders of the people. But at length, with Joshua, he trod the soil of the Promised Land!

When Joshua was dividing the land, Caleb went to him and reminded him of the promise of God, and how he had wholly followed the Lord his God. "The Lord," he said, "hath kept me alive, as he said, these forty and five years. . . . And now, lo, I am this day fourscore and five years old. As yet I am as strong this day as I was in the day that Moses sent me: as my strength was then, even so is my strength now, for war, both to go out, and to come in." And for what part of the land did Caleb ask? What part of the conquest did he ask Joshua to assign to him? Why, that very part of the land where the sons of Anak, the giants, lived, the stronghold of Hebron! This was the difficult task for which the octogenarian Caleb asked. And this was the land that he conquered! Caleb did not ask to be retired because he was eighty-five years of age. Like Moses, his eye was not dim nor his natural force abated. At eighty-five he still had that magnificent spirit of courage which he had at forty, when he brought in his report concerning the Promised Land, and, in spite of fierce tribesmen, walled cities, and huge giants, said, "Let us go up at once and possess it."

Such, then, is the story of the man who wholly followed the Lord his God—the man who saw the walled cities, the Hittites, the Amalekites, the Amorites, the Jebusites, but also the presence and the power of God.

> Have you come to the Red Sea place in your life,
> Where, in spite of all you can do,
> There is no way out, there is no way back,

There is no other way but through?
Then wait on the Lord with a trust serene
  Till the night of your fear is gone;
He will send the winds, He will heap the floods,
  When He says to your soul, "Go on!" [1]

When Christian, in *Pilgrim's Progress*, reached the top of the Hill Difficulty, he came upon two men "running amain," whose names were Timorous and Mistrust. Christian said to them, "Sirs, what's the matter? You run the wrong way."

Timorous answered that they were going to the city of Zion, "but the farther we go, the more danger we meet with; wherefore we turned, and are going back again."

And Mistrust said: "Just before us lie a couple of lions in the way, whether sleeping or waking we know not; and we could not think, if we came within reach, but they would presently pull us in pieces."

But Christian wisely replied: "You make me afraid; but whither shall I fly to be safe? If I go back to my own country, that is prepared for fire and brimstone, and I shall certainly perish there; if I can get to the Celestial City, I am sure to be in safety there: I must venture. To go back is nothing but death; to go forward is fear of death, and life everlasting beyond it. I will yet go forward."

There are many lions and giants in your path on the way to the Celestial City: lions and giants of fear and pride and covetousness and doubt and evil passions. You cannot get to the Celestial City without meeting them and

---

[1] Annie Johnson Flint. "At the Place of the Sea." By permission of Evangelical Publishers, Toronto, Canada.

conquering them. But that can be done! To go back is death! To go forward in the power of Christ is eternal life. Look, therefore, unto Jesus, the captain of your salvation, the author and finisher of your faith, and remember that "greater is he that is in you, than he that is in the world."

VI

EZEKIEL—THE MAN OF SORROW AND OF VISION

"The Lord is there."

Ezek. 48:35

"THE LORD IS THERE." THAT IS THE FINAL SENTENCE in one of the greatest books of the Bible, and that is the last word of one of the greatest men of the Bible, the prophet Ezekiel. At the end of this strange and wonderful book, with its visions of glory, with its predictions of battles and slaughters, with its strange symbols and extraordinary dramas, and soaring eloquence—at the end of it all comes this sentence, "The Lord is there." The book concludes with a vision of a marvelous city, as large as Palestine itself, and a temple of God as large as Jerusalem, and of this city and temple it is written, "The Lord is there."

"The Lord is there." Any prophet, any preacher, any teacher, any book, any picture, any providence or experience in life which can say that to you, which can tell you that life is more than meat and the body more than raiment, which can persuade you that life has spiritual outgoings, that the destiny of the soul is something more than just a struggle in the darkness in the defiles of this world's wilderness, and after that the silence—any book, any friend, prophet, teacher, preacher, experience which can say that to you, "The Lord is there," is well worthy of your attention.

The book of Ezekiel is one of the grandest, but most

difficult and obscure, of all the books of the Bible; but in it there are flashes of unsurpassed beauty and splendor. The prophet Ezekiel is one of those men who can say to their fellow men, "The Lord is there"; one of those dead, but sceptred spirits, the real sovereigns of the world, "who rule us from their urns." Ezekiel was a contemporary of the prophet Jeremiah; but while Jeremiah prophesied during the sunset of the Hebrew monarchy at Jerusalem, Ezekiel prophesied to the Jews who already had been carried into the land of captivity.

EZEKIEL'S COMPASSION AND SYMPATHY

The captives from Jerusalem were settled along the banks of the River Chebar, a hundred or more miles up the Euphrates from Babylon. Ezekiel tells us that he went and shared the hardships and the captivity of his people. "I sat where they sat." He was to deliver a stern message of judgment and retribution, and his face was to be adamant against his own people. But like his great contemporary Jeremiah, he was a man of compassion and sympathy. "I sat where they sat."

Compassion and sympathy are a fountain whence have flowed the rivers of influence which have come from the noblest lives. Moses might have chosen to be called the son of Pharaoh's daughter, and shared the ease and splendor of the court of the Pharaohs; but when he saw an Egyptian smiting one of his brethren, a Hebrew, he was moved with compassion, and smote him and delivered him. That was one of the reasons why God called him to deliver his people. There is an old Roman proverb, "If you would make me weep, you must first weep yourself."

Another great deliverer and builder of Israel was Nehemiah. When he received word at the court of Persia, where he was a cupbearer to the despot Artaxerxes, of the sad ruin of Jerusalem, his heart was so filled with sorrow that his face reflected that sorrow as he stood before the king with the royal cup in his hand, and the king asked him the cause of his sorrow. Then Nehemiah answered: "Why should not my countenance be sad, when the city, the place of my fathers' sepulchres, lieth waste, and the gates thereof are consumed with fire?" It was the sorrow and compassion of Nehemiah that moved the heart of Artaxerxes to permit Nehemiah to return to Jerusalem to rebuild its walls. The builders of the world are always men who care.

When Tiberius Gracchus, on a journey from Spain to Rome, was passing through the fields of Etruria, he was shocked and pained to see the condition of the slaves who were toiling in the fields. It was that vision of the sufferings of the common people and the laboring classes which led him to inaugurate one of the greatest of social revolutions.

Once, on a midnight visit to a police station in Edinburgh, a young Scottish preacher, afterwards famous, Thomas Guthrie, saw the homeless waifs who had come there to seek shelter. On an open space before the stove, where the light shone full on his face, lay a little lad who attracted his special attention. The boy was about eight years old, but with a sweet and innocent face; "his pillow a brick, and as he lay calm in sleep, forgetful of his sorrows, he might have served for a picture of injured innocence. He knew neither father nor mother, brothers nor friend. In the wide world his only friends were the police. How he lived they did not know. But there he was at night." Guthrie said that for days and nights he could not get that boy out of his mind or heart. It was scenes like this which moved him to inaugurate his great work for the guarding and reformation of the outcast children of Edinburgh. Today on beautiful Princes Street you can see the monument of the great preacher, with the "street Arabs" taking refuge under his arm. "I have the satisfaction," said Guthrie, "when I lay my head upon my pillow of always finding one part of it soft, and that is that God has made me an instrument in his hands by saving many a poor creature from a life of misery and crime."

Let us keep our hearts soft and tender like the Master whose name we profess. Let us be moved with compassion, and ever ask his Holy Spirit to teach us to "feel another's woe." Because he "sat where they sat," Ezekiel was called to his high office.

EZEKIEL'S DEVOTION TO THE WILL OF GOD

Before Ezekiel commenced to speak to the people he was given a prophetic roll to eat. This, no doubt, was in a vision; but it was a vision which symbolized his complete devotion to the will of God, and to the word of God. Like Jeremiah, he could say: "His word was in mine heart as a burning fire shut up in my bones, and I was weary with forbearing, and I could not stay."

Another proof in the life of Ezekiel of his complete devotion to God's word and will was his conduct at the time of the death of his wife. The word of God came to him saying, "Son of man, behold, I take away from thee the desire of thine eyes with a stroke: yet neither shalt thou mourn nor weep, neither shall thy tears run down." His tearless sorrow was to be a sign to the people that the calamity which was to overtake Jerusalem would be so great that no sorrow could measure it. It was to be a woe the depth of which could not be expressed in mourning.

His wife, "the desire" of his eyes, died; but true to the command of the Lord, in the morning Ezekiel did as God commanded. "At even my wife died; and I did in the morning as I was commanded." He says nothing of what took place that night between the last ray of light and the first beams of the morning: the tumult of emotion, the vain appeals, the groping hand stretched through the night. Of all this there is not an echo; but in the morning we see him standing, girded for his task, obedient unto God, master of his grief and master of himself. "I did in the morning as I was commanded."

In this instance we have a very lofty example of the subordination of domestic sorrow to public service. Ezekiel suffered, but he realized that his nation was greater than he was, that his own sorrows must be drowned in the sorrows of his people and his country. Our own American history has an example of that which compels our admiration and touches our hearts. During the dark days of the first years of the war, Lincoln's heart was lightened by the pranks and romping of his two younger sons William and Thomas, who kept the White House in joyous uproar. But early in February, 1862, William sickened and died. For a time Lincoln was almost inconsolable in his sorrow, and his friends had to remonstrate with him when he fell into the habit of observing the Thursday on which the child died as a day of sorrow and retirement. But soon the president mastered his sorrow, and although he wore his sackcloth, like the king on the walls of Samaria, he wore his sackcloth within. Now and then we have an intimation of his struggle and his grief; but the nation itself saw nothing of that. Armies and fleets had to be dispatched, defeated generals encouraged, foolish and incompetent ones replaced, and the heart of the nation strengthened in the Lord. His own private sorrow was subordinated to the state. At even his son died, but in the morning, the morning of duty which waits us all, he did as God commanded. The victory of Ezekiel was won by the recognition of that which is greater than man's joys or man's sorrows or man's ambitions, and that is man's duty. God was first in the life of this man. He was absolutely devoted to the word of the Lord.

EZEKIEL'S VISION OF THE GLORY OF GOD IN HISTORY

Such then was the man to whom was granted an overwhelming vision of the glory of God. On the banks of the Chebar, Ezekiel saw a whirlwind circled with coruscations of fire. Out of the whirlwind emerged the four living creatures with four faces, the face of a man, a lion, an ox, and an eagle. The living creatures which ran with outstretched wings were attended by four great wheels. These wheels moved with the living creatures, not only forward, but backward, and to either side, and the rims of the wheels, high and dreadful, were full of eyes. Above the living creatures was the likeness of a sapphire throne, and upon the throne was the appearance of a man which was the appearance of the glory of the Lord.

This magnificent vision has always been taken to express not only the majesty and the glory of God, but the sovereignty of God, his activity in history, and his rule among men and nations.

The rims of the wheels were full of eyes. This expresses God's perfect knowledge and the absolute wisdom and justice of his doings. At first glance the history of the world seems to be just a rush and a roar and a flash of the wheels of events, getting nowhere, guided by no intelligence, accomplishing no great end. We seem to see nothing but the monotonous cycle of war and invasion, the rise and fall of empires, one crowding another down into its grave. But when we look at history in the light of the truth of God's government, we discern something more than chaos and confusion. We discover that these ever-turning and ever-flashing wheels of the world's events are full of the eyes of intelligent purpose, and that just as the movement of the four living creatures and the four wheels was sometimes backward, and sometimes to either side, and yet ever straight forward, so the chariot of divine Providence moves ever onward to its great goal.

The vision of Ezekiel, or the glory of God in history and in providence, is one which gives us strength and hope in such an age as this. Amid the thunders of war and the horrors of battle in the air, on the land, on the sea, and under the sea, and amid the invasion and destruction of the weaker nations, it reminds us that God is on his throne, that he doeth his will in the armies of heaven and among the inhabitants of the earth, and that through all the perplexing happenings of this troubled world the chariot of the divine Purpose moves steadily forward. Ezekiel says that about the throne of God there was a rainbow. The rainbow of God's mercy encircles all the events of history, and in the end, out of it all, shall come that redeemed society, of which it shall be possible to say, "The Lord is there."

EZEKIEL'S VISION OF THE FUTURE

Not only was Ezekiel given the assurance of God's power and glory in the events of the world, but he was given a vision of the future blessedness which is to descend upon mankind. This vision took the form of a great city and a great temple. Accompanied by a heavenly guide, Ezekiel in his vision sees a stream of water issuing from the foundations of the temple and flowing eastward. A short distance from the temple the angel measured the waters, and the waters were only to the ankles. Still further on he measured them again, and the waters were up to the knees of Ezekiel as he passed through them. Again he measured them, and the waters were up to his loins. And then a final measure, when he found a river too deep to ford, a river to swim in. As he followed the course of the river he marked the many trees with their greenness and shade which grew on either side of the river. Wherever the river flowed, there was vegetation and life. He could follow the river as it flowed eastward by the trail of green, here dark and deep, and there fresh and tender, which it left behind it. "Everything shall live whither the river cometh." Even the Dead Sea, that monster among inland seas, heavy with salt, more than a thousand feet below the level of the ocean, with no outlet, and its bituminous waters scarcely tolerating any forms of life, was healed by the templeborn river which emptied a pure life-giving stream into its bosom.

This is a vision. It is hardly a real river which Ezekiel is describing, but a river which in its origin, its gradual increase, its universal benediction, is a symbol of the power and blessedness of true religion. To us today that mystic river is a parable of the origin, the increase and the blessings and the glory of the Church of Christ and the River of Life with which it has watered the earth. Here was a river which had a divine origin. Our faith is the "glorious gospel of the blessed God." It is not anything that man discovered for himself. By its own wisdom the world knew not God, and it pleased God, by the foolishness of preaching, to save them that believe. Eye had not seen, ear heard, neither had entered into the heart of man, the things which God had prepared for them that love him; but God in the fullness of time revealed them unto us by his Spirit.

The mystic river of Ezekiel's vision gradually grew in width and depth from a river that was only up to the ankles to a river to swim in. There was nothing unusual about that. That is the way all rivers increase in volume and in depth as they flow farther away from their source. But in the rivers of the earth that increase in depth and volume is not due to the flow of the river at its source and supply. Rivers increase by reason of the tributary streams which empty their waters into them as they flow seaward. I have seen the Mississippi River, the Father of Waters, as a little stream in Minnesota, and I have crossed its immense and tawny flood at New Orleans; but that enormous increase in volume is not to be accounted for by the flow of that fountain lake in the far north, but by the tributary streams which have lost themselves in the Mississippi— the Fox, the Wisconsin, the Miami, the Muskingum, the Allegheny, the Monongahela, and the Ohio. These are the rivers that make the Mississippi great. But this stream of the prophet's vision was fed by no waters save those which issued from beneath the temple. Here we have the parable of the truth that the growth and the future conquest of Christianity are not due to human enterprise and effort, but to the mighty impulse which lies at its origin, in the redeeming purpose and sacrificial love of God. Christianity has given light to the world, but it has borrowed none. Not an age, not a race, not a single person, even so gifted and powerful a personality as

Paul, has added anything to the power and content of Christian truth.

The templeborn river of Ezekiel's vision is a parable not only of the origin and the growth of Christianity, but of the blessings which it has bestowed, and which it will yet bestow. As you can trace the course of a river across the desert by the fringe of green, so you can trace the course of the gospel in the world by the reformations which it has effected and the deserts which it has reclaimed and the dead seas which it has healed. "Every thing shall live whither the river cometh."

> Blessings abound where e'r He reigns,
> The prisoner leaps to lose his chains;
> The weary find eternal rest,
> And all the sons of want are blessed.

The river that flowed from the temple reclaimed the desert and healed the Dead Sea. So our faith, resting not upon man, and not upon what we see about us in the world today, looks confidently forward to the day when the river that flowed from the foot of the cross of Christ shall fill the whole earth, reclaim every desert and make it blossom like the rose, and heal every dead sea of man's hatred and sin, and war and bitterness and strife. Ezekiel saluted that day with the closing sentence of his prophecy, "The Lord is there." It was the same vision, the same assurance that Paul gave when, in his great inspired vision, he saluted the end of the ages, when Christ, having put all enemies under his feet, even the last enemy, which is death, and having delivered up the Kingdom to God, even the Father, God shall be all and in all.

What the River of Salvation, the gospel of Christ, will

do for the world, it can do for you. You need not wait for the end of the ages to experience the healing power of this divine river of faith and life. It can water and cause to bring forth those areas in your life which now are desert, where no good or beautiful thing grows; it can heal and take the poison out of every dead sea of sin in the human heart. It can produce that most beautiful object under the sun, a Christian man or woman, of whose life and thought and deeds it is possible to say, "The Lord is there."

VII

CORNELIUS—A GOOD SOLDIER OF JESUS CHRIST

"Who shall tell thee words, whereby thou and all thy house shall be saved."

Acts 11:14

GOD SOMETIMES MOVES IN A MYSTERIOUS WAY TO PER-form the wonders of his grace. The story of the conversion of the Roman officer Cornelius fixes our attention not only upon the fact that this soldier bowed at the feet of the Prince of Peace, but also upon the wonderful way in which he was brought to hear of the gospel. The story of his conversion naturally divides itself into three parts: first, the congregation and the preacher, and the way in which they were brought together; second, the sermon which was preached; and third, the results of the sermon and its far-reaching implications.

THE CONGREGATION AND THE PREACHER

Cornelius was a centurion; that is, the commander of the sixtieth part of a Roman legion, or one hundred men. He was stationed at Caesarea, which was the seat of the Roman government in that part of Syria. His company, perhaps made up of crack troops, was known as the Italian Band. All the associations and all the environment of Cornelius were against his being a good man and a man of faith. He had an official post in a day of unspeak-able licentiousness and corruption. His business was that of war. Yet, so placed, Cornelius was a good man. Too

[80]

much is made today of heredity and environment, and too many faults and transgressions are condoned or excused on their account. There are indeed some people so situated that religious faith and character, humanly speaking, seems unlikely, if not impossible; whereas others are so situated that good character and religious faith would seem to be almost inevitable. Yet there are plenty of instances where men have failed utterly in spite of a favorable environment; and other instances where men have come to nobility of character and greatness of faith in spite of very unfavorable environment. Joseph, in the house of Potiphar, did not sink to the low level of that house, but rose far above it, like a star over the ocean. Obadiah, in the house of Ahab and Jezebel, did not yield to his environment and become a prophet of Baal, but remained a prophet of the true God. Daniel, in the court of Nebuchadnezzar, defiled neither his body with the king's meat nor his soul with the customs of that wicked court; and when Paul preached the gospel at Rome, there were saints in Caesar's household.

In spite of his official position and all the temptations that went with it, Cornelius appears before us as a devout man and one who feared God with all his house, who gave much alms to the people, and prayed to God always. He was therefore a just man, charitable, devout, and prayerful. One day at the ninth hour, as he was praying, an angel of God came to him and said, "Cornelius!" The devout aspirations of Cornelius had no doubt prepared his soul to receive a special revelation. The great movements in a work of conversion are all on God's side. The truth is generally revealed like a flash of light; yet it is revealed to those who have, all unknown to themselves, for a long time been preparing to receive that revelation. Nor need we wonder that in this case God made use of dreams or visions. Shakespeare in several cases puts the deepest moral experiences of bad men and bad women into their dreams. Why therefore should it be thought strange that the greatest moral experience of good men should have come to them in their dreams?

The angel assured Cornelius that his prayers and his alms had not been unnoted of God. He said to him, "Thy prayer is heard." We take from this that Cornelius had been praying for a higher religious experience, a closer approach to God, and a deeper sense of peace and forgiveness. Here Christ answers his own great beatitude, "Blessed are they which do hunger and thirst after righteousness: for they shall be filled."

Cornelius is directed to send messengers to Joppa, where they are to ask for one Simon, surnamed Peter, who was lodging in the house of Simon the tanner, by the seaside. Peter, said the angel, "shall tell thee words whereby thou and all thy house shall be saved." Nothing doubting, and yet perhaps wondering what it all meant, Cornelius dispatched two servants, together with a trusted soldier, to go to Joppa and ask for Peter.

Now the scene shifts from Caesarea to Joppa. At the sixth hour Peter goes up on the housetop to pray. From his place of prayer he can see the sleeping sea, the flat-roofed houses of Joppa, and the hills beyond. It was some time since Peter had eaten, and he became very hungry. While he was waiting he fell into a trance. In his vision he saw heaven open, and a great sheet, in which were all manner of animals and creeping things and fowls of the air, was let down to the earth. Then he heard a voice saying, "Rise, Peter; kill, and eat." But Peter responded, "Not so, Lord; for I have never eaten any thing that is common or unclean." How characteristic that answer is of Peter; a strange combination of devotion and worship, and yet self-will and disobedience. It is a note which we hear echoing all through the great apostle's life. When Jesus, after Peter had acknowledged him to be the Son of God, told his disciples of the humiliation and death of the cross, Peter began to rebuke him saying, "Lord, this shall not be unto thee." So even down to the time of his great apostolic ministry, Peter is the man who will call Jesus, "Lord," and yet question his commandments.

Three times the sheet was let down and then drawn up into heaven, while a voice said, "What God hath cleansed, that call not thou common." Peter, now awakened out of his dream, was wondering what it all meant when he heard the knocking on the door of Simon by the three messengers who had come from Cornelius. When he went down to them the messengers told him that they had been sent by Cornelius to bring him to their master. The next day Peter went with them, and at Caesarea was greeted by Cornelius who fell at his feet to worship him. Peter told him to stand up, saying, "I myself also am a man," with the inference that God alone was worthy of worship. As if to excuse himself for his presence in this pagan company, Peter said to Cornelius and his family and neighbors who also had come in, that although it was unlawful for a Jew to keep company with men of other nations, God had showed him that He was not to be bound any longer by such customs or prejudices. Then he asks Cornelius what he wants. Cornelius tells the story of his vision, and then says to Peter, "Now therefore are we all here present before God, to hear all things that are commanded thee of God." When a congregation and a minister meet on that footing, a minister like Peter, who comes, not to air his own fancies, but to speak the things commanded him of God, and a congregation like Cornelius, ready and willing to hear what God will say, then we may expect the blessing of the Holy Spirit.

THE SERMON

Then Peter opened his mouth and commenced with a declaration which has been often and sadly misinterpreted: "Of a truth I perceive that God is no respecter of persons; but in every nation he that feareth him, and worketh righteousness is accepted with him." This has been strangely distorted to mean that if one lives a good decent life, is honest, charitable, even religiously inclined, he can get along without the gospel and without Christ. But this misses the point altogether. What Peter meant was that through the agency of his dream it had been brought home to him that the gospel of Christ was not intended for those only who are of the Jewish race, but was to be preached to men of every race and every speech, for their souls too were dear to God.

With that great introduction Peter preached his memorable sermon. What do you think he said to this centurion? He might have eulogized him for his generosity and justice and purity of life; but if he had done so, I fancy I can see the countenance of the centurion fall, for with all his attainments in the path of virtue, there was in the centurion's heart a deep longing for peace and a happiness which thus far had eluded him. Or if Peter had not known about the man's character, suppose he had reasoned with him of righteousness and temperance and exhorted him to be a kind, just, religious, and prayerful man? Then too I think I can see the centurion's countenance fall. All of this he had striven to be, and yet he was not satisfied; not satisfied either with the progress he had made or with the blessedness that such progress had brought to him. But here was a preacher who did not disappoint his congregation. He preached Jesus to the centurion as Philip had preached Jesus to the Ethiopian. He told him of the life of Jesus, how he was full of the Holy Ghost, and went about doing good and healing all that were oppressed of the devil. Then he told him of his crucifixion, how they slew him and hanged him on a tree. But how on the third day God raised him up, and he appeared alive, not to the people generally, but to witnesses who had known him before and who were qualified to testify of what they had seen and heard. Then he tells Cornelius, having thus given him the foundation facts of the gospel, what message this Jesus commanded his disciples to preach to the world. First, that to him all the prophets had witnessed. Christ was not an accident upon the field of time, but he came in the fullness of time and in fulfillment of God's great plan to redeem the world. Second, that Christ is ordained of God to be the judge of the quick and the dead, that before him who is both the world's Saviour and Judge, all men, the Jew and the Gentile, the Roman and the barbarian, the quick and the dead, the harlot and the saint, the thief and the devout centurion, must stand to give their account. And third, that through faith in his name men may receive the remission of their sins. This was the sermon which Peter preached to the centurion, and preached according to the commandment of the risen Jesus himself. If you want to know what Jesus desires his Church to say of him, read that last part of the tenth chapter of Acts. Would to God that all of us preachers could be as faithful to Christ's commandments as Peter was in this great sermon on this great occasion which marked the expansion of Christianity from a narrow sect to a world conquering faith.

THE SERMON'S RESULTS AND IMPLICATIONS

At the end of Peter's sermon, the Holy Ghost fell on all them that heard the Word. In this case the gift of the Holy Spirit was accompanied by that mysterious sign, the speaking with tongues. But we must not permit the obscurity of that gift to hide from us what the great work of the Holy Spirit here was—repentance and faith in the Lord Jesus Christ. Such a sermon as Peter preached is the only kind of a sermon which can produce repentance and faith. It may not always do it, for the Spirit, like the wind, bloweth where it listeth. Nevertheless it is the *only kind* of a sermon which *can* produce repentance and faith. It did so in this case. Cornelius gave such evidence of his faith and repentance that Peter himself proposed to him baptism, as the confirmation of his faith and his introduction into the Church of Jesus Christ. Peter did not stop by congratulating the centurion upon his faith and repentance, but told him to be baptized. Peter was not wiser than his Lord, who told his disciples to preach the gospel unto every creature, saying, "He that believeth and is baptized shall be saved." "If thou shalt confess with thy mouth the Lord Jesus, and shalt believe in thine heart that God hath raised him from the dead, thou shalt be saved. For with the heart man believeth unto righteousness; and with the mouth confession is made unto salvation."

The question is often asked—indeed it seems to have been asked from the very beginning—Does a moral man need a Redeemer? That question, it seems to me, was answered clearly and once for all in the conversion of this first man from the Gentile world. It is worth remembering that he was not a drunkard or thief or libertine, but the very pick of the pagan world, just, devout, and charitable. When Peter arrived in Caesarea I can imagine him asking some man in the street where Cornelius lived, and that man inquiring of Peter what his business might be with Cornelius, and Peter responding, "I go to preach the gospel to Cornelius; to tell him how Christ died for sinners on the cross, and that through faith in him men have the forgiveness of their sins." But the man answers: "It must be some other Cornelius whom you are looking for. There is a notorious brigand in the jail just now. Perhaps he is the man. But certainly not the Roman centurion. Why, you are only wasting your efforts in preaching to him. The Gentiles honor him, the Jews respect him, the soldiers adore him, widows and orphans rise up to call him blessed, and I am told that he spends a good part of every day in pious meditation and prayer. Tell this gospel of yours with its message of salvation from sin to some of the drunken legionnaires who are stationed here, or to some of the cruel publicans who grind the face of the poor, or tell it to the harlots or the menstealers; tell it—let me whisper it—to our dissipated Governor Felix, and his Drusilla, but not to that good man Cornelius."

Yet in all that pagan world, so sunken in debauchery and sins unmentionable, it is to this devout Roman soldier that the Holy Ghost directs the apostle to preach the gospel of repentance and salvation. If a man like Cornelius needed to repent and be saved, then what shall we say for ourselves? Yet the question will always be asked, although God answered it so plainly in the conversion of Cornelius.

[87]

One says that he is a member of the lodge, and that the principles which it inculcates seem to be much the same as the principles of Christianity, indeed, are based upon it. Or another describes a man who is interested in every good work, who stands for the highest things in the community, gives to every good cause, and is a good husband and father in his home. Is not this sufficient? Not if the conversion of Cornelius is a true fact and was inspired by the Holy Ghost, because it tells us plainly that a man can be a good citizen, an honest man, a charitable man, just in his dealings, a good husband or father or son, and yet lack the one great thing. If repentance and salvation were preached to a man like Cornelius, then every man needs to repent and be saved.

Most of us will not have much difficulty in this matter because we can hardly claim the moral standing of Cornelius, and if a man like him had to repent, and needed salvation through the shed blood of Christ, then what of us? In the introduction to his *Confessions,* Rousseau commences with these striking words:

Such as I was I have declared myself to be, sometimes vile and despicable; at others, virtuous, generous and sublime. Even as thou hast read my inmost soul, Power Eternal assemble round thy throne an innumerable throng of my fellow mortals. Let them listen to my confessions, let them blush at my depravity, let them tremble at my sufferings, let each in his turn expose with equal sincerity the failings, the wanderings of his heart, and, if he dare, aver, "I was better than that man."

Who here tonight cares to accept that challenge?

Cornelius now passes from the New Testament stage.

But in heaven he is glad to take his place in the company of redeemed souls and, standing side by side with Mary of Magdala and the penitent thief, sing with them, his face, I think, not less radiant than theirs, the song of redemption, "Unto him that loved us, and washed us from our sins in his own blood."

VIII

MARK—THE MAN WHO FAILED AND THEN MADE GOOD

> "John departing from them returned
> to Jerusalem."
>
> ACTS 13:13
>
> "Take Mark, and bring him with thee:
> for he is profitable to me for the ministry."
>
> II TIM. 4:11

THIS IS A SERMON FOUND WHERE ALL TRUE SERMONS are found—in the Bible. But the power of it, the charm of it, and the timeliness of it were brought vividly to my mind one summer in my travels in the footsteps of Paul.

After our ship left the Island of Cyprus at Limassol, we sailed around the western end of Cyprus, and then straight north to Antalya in Turkey, on the southern shore of Asia Minor. Antalya is situated on the great Bay of Antalya, one of the remarkable geographical features of Asia Minor. For hours your ship is sailing into this bay, which cuts its way deep into Asia Minor, and on either side of you, as you look to the east and to the west, are the great yellow mountains which are so familiar a part of the landscape in that part of the world.

This was the route followed by Paul and Barnabas on the first missionary journey. They had sailed from Seleucia, the port of Antioch, and landing at Cyprus at Salamis, had traveled through the island to Paphos, where they took ship for Asia Minor. They landed in this same Bay of Antalya at Perga, a considerable city of Pamphylia. Perga is now a desolation. But the other port, Attalia, just near to Perga, from which the apostles sailed on their return voyage, is still a considerable city. It is picturesquely located on high cliffs. The town is blessed with the plentiful waters of the river Cataractes, which flows down from the mountains and falls in beautiful cascades over the cliff into the sea. There are some Roman ruins in the town, and a few towers and walls dating back to the days of the Venetians. The town shows the scars of bombardment by Italian warships during World War I.

As our ship sailed into this remarkable bay, and as I walked along the cliffs at Antalya and looked at the great mountains beyond the Pamphylian plain, I was thinking not only of Paul and his noble companion Barnabas, but in a very special way of their companion and helper John Mark. John Mark was the nephew of Barnabas, a prominent citizen of Cyprus, who was converted to Christianity and devoted his goods as well as his life to the cause of Christ. Mark's mother, possibly the sister of Barnabas, was the Mary of whom we read in Acts, at whose wealthy home the apostles were wont to meet, and where Peter went after he had been released from Herod's prison. When Paul and Barnabas returned from Jerusalem to Antioch after their errand in the interests of the poor of Jerusalem, they were accompanied by Mark, and when the apostles were solemnly ordained to go forth on the work to which the Holy Spirit had called them, they took with them as their minister or helper John Mark.

Mark accompanied them to Cyprus, through the island of Cyprus, and then across the sea to Perga on the Bay of Antalya. Then we come to the brief statement of Luke that at that place John Mark deserted them and went back to Jerusalem. From the attitude which Paul later took we know that there was no good excuse for this turning back of Mark. Where Luke is silent we can only guess at the reasons for Mark's action. Possibly the young man had become homesick. Perhaps the early zeal with which he started out had flagged, and the whole expedition had become distasteful to him. Perhaps he had been seasick on the voyage from Cyprus. Perhaps he had been bitten by the numerous insects, and had been attacked with the malaria that is still prevalent in Pamphylia. Perhaps he took a look at the grim Taurus Mountains, or heard a rumor of the brigands and robber tribes which roamed through the mountains which lay between Pamphylia and Galatia. Paul was now getting into difficult and dangerous territory, and beginning to write the history of what he calls "perils of waters, . . . of robbers, . . . by mine own countrymen, . . . by the heathen, . . . in the city, . . . in the wilderness, . . . in the sea, . . . among false brethren." Probably Mark saw what was coming. He didn't have the stuff in him to face it or endure it. He left the elderly Barnabas and the frail Paul to climb the mountain passes by themselves and took the first ship back to Syria.

When Paul and Barnabas were planning the next great journey and were ready to start from Antioch, Barnabas wanted to take Mark, who by this time had rejoined them. But Paul refused to let Mark accompany them, deeming it not right or wise to take with them a man who had turned back just when the dangers were commencing on the previous journey. This led to a sad dispute between Paul and Barnabas, and to the separation of those two great men. Paul took Silas and starting northward went to Tarsus and through the Cilician Gates into Galatia;

while Barnabas took Mark, and going down to Seleucia, sailed again for Cyprus.

Standing on the rocks of the ancient quay at Seleucia, you see in your imagination that ship sailing westward to Cyprus, with Barnabas and Mark on board. But how different this voyage is for Mark. On the previous voyage Paul had been with them, and Mark was full of courage and zeal and hope. Now they sail without Paul, because Paul regarded Mark as a quitter, a coward, and a deserter, not fit to go with him on the great journey into Asia.

That is the last we see of Mark for some time. He is the man who has failed, and failed about as miserably as anyone could fail. Men will forgive almost any fault or weakness but that of cowardice, and that was the charge against Mark. The bravest soul that the world ever saw had told Mark that he was not fit to go with him on his dangerous journey to the heathen.

But that is not the whole story of Mark. If it were, he would not be worth preaching about. There is another and a better chapter in Mark's history. The next time we hear of him he is in the company of the other great figure among the apostles, Peter. In his first epistle Peter sends a message to the Christians persecuted and scattered in the world and says, "The church that is at Babylon"— probably the name he gave to Rome—"saluteth you, and so doth Marcus my son." By that time, then, Mark had so approved himself in the eyes of Peter that he was with him as a companion and friend. Paul calls Timothy "my son." So Peter speaks of Mark as his son. Evidently there is complete confidence and deep affection in his relationship with Mark. The Gospel According to Mark, by an almost universal tradition, is attributed to this relationship between Peter and Mark. The vivid and graphic style of the second Gospel is understandable when we remember that Mark is relating what Peter, an eyewitness, told him.

The next mention of Mark is also from Rome. But this time we find Mark not with Peter but with Paul. In his letter to the Colossians, Paul sends this greeting: "Aristarchus my fellow prisoner saluteth you, and Marcus, sister's son to Barnabas, . . . if he come unto you, receive him." By this time Mark had completely re-established himself in the opinion of Paul. The message to the Church to receive Mark seems to have back of it the thought that Mark's reputation as a deserter and quitter had gone before him in the Church, and Paul wants to make sure that they will not now hold this against him. Again, at the end of the letter to Philemon, Paul sends to Philemon the greetings of Mark, Aristarchus, Demas, and Luke, his fellow workers.

But the most thrilling and the most moving mention of Mark is in Paul's last letter, the second letter to Timothy, not long before his death. In the cold and damp Mamertine dungeon Paul wrote his letter, perhaps by the hand of Luke, to Timothy at Ephesus, telling him to bring his cloak that he had left behind at Troas, the books and the parchments. He wants Timothy to come, and to come before winter, for he says, "Demas hath forsaken me, . . . and is departed unto Thessalonica, Crescens to Galatia, Titus unto Dalmatia. Only Luke is with me." Then Paul adds another request. There is another friend whom he wants to have by his side in this last hour. Who, I wonder, will that friend be? Onesimus, whom he had rescued from sin and shame? Aristarchus, or Silas, the companion of his journeys? Epaphroditus, who had come from Philippi on an earlier imprisonment to minister to Paul?

Epaphras from Colossae, who also had come during the first imprisonment to help Paul at Rome? Priscilla and Aquilla? Tertius? Tychicus, the brother beloved? No, none of these. This was the message Paul wrote; this was the man whom he desired to have at his side in the last great hour, with death's shadows coming down— "Take Mark, and bring him with thee: for he is profitable to me for the ministry." It was as if he said: "As I go to face the Roman lion I want Mark—Mark, who deserted me at Perga and left Barnabas and me to climb the mountain passes by ourselves and face the perils of robbers and the mobs of Antioch and Lystra and Iconium; Mark, the quitter and the coward; Mark, who separated me from Barnabas, the man in all the world to whom I owed the most—bring him with thee, for he is profitable to me in the ministry!"

Mark, who started so poorly, made a grand finish. He threw away his first chance, but he made noble use of his second chance. He who appears at first in the sacred narrative as a coward and deserter is mentioned at the end of Paul's life as the man he wants by his side as he faces death at the hand of Nero. The man of weakness and of cowardice became the man who wrote the great second Gospel, the man whose symbol is the lion.

What were the elements and factors in the recovery of Mark? First of all there was his own determination to make good where he had failed. When some men are rebuked for their weakness and their failure, and as severely as Paul rebuked Mark when he refused to let him be in his company even on the second journey, the result often is a spirit of defiance and anger that leads them into the deeper dishonor. But with Mark it was the reverse. Instead of being angry with Paul, instead of defiantly abandoning

[95]

Christianity, Mark resolved in his heart that he would show Paul that he could make a man out of himself yet.

When Andrew D. White, once ambassador to Germany, and formerly president of Cornell University, commenced his teaching career at the University of Michigan, he was greatly annoyed by an able but impudent and disorderly student in one of his classes. He managed to win the friendship of this student, who, however, was later dismissed from the university for participation in a disgraceful escapade in which one of the students was killed. Before he left the university this student came to see White to thank him for what he had tried to do for him. As he was leaving, he said, "I'll make a man out of myself yet." The Civil War was just breaking out, and the expelled student enlisted in a Michigan calvary regiment. On the third day of the Battle of Gettysburg, in the new uniform of a brigadier general, to which rank he had just been promoted for fidelity and gallantry, an officer was ordered by General Kilpatrick to charge the right wing of the Confederate army. It was a mistaken order. But leading his men in a magnificent but hopeless charge, the young officer fell gloriously within the Confederate lines. It was General E. J. Farnsworth, the student who had been expelled from the University of Michigan. He had made good his promise that he would make a man out of himself. No matter what the mistakes or failures or blunders, there is the possibility of noble and honorable success, if the will and the purpose are there.

Another element in the restoration of Mark was the kindness and sympathy of Peter. After all, it was not strange that Peter was so kind to Mark and sympathized with him, for Peter himself could look back to that dark, dark, bitter hour, when he went out and wept bitterly after he had denied his Lord and failed him so terribly in his hour of need. Yes, Peter could well sympathize with Mark.

Then we must give Paul credit too. Many a man of lesser parts would never have been reconciled to one who had deserted him in the hour of need as Mark had done at Perga. But it was a matter of principle with Paul, not a matter of personal feeling, and the moment Mark proved that he could do better than he did at Perga, and that he wanted to do better, Paul gave him his chance. It was Paul, you know, who wrote those beautiful words: "Brethren, if a man be overtaken in a fault, ye who are spiritual, restore such a one, . . . considering thyself, lest thou also be tempted." In the case of Mark, Paul practiced what he preached. He told Mark that all had been forgiven, and all would be forgotten. There is something wonderfully beautiful in that request of Paul that Timothy, when he came from Asia, should bring with him to be by his side in the last darkness the very man who had deserted him and forsaken him at the foot of the Galatian mountains.

But most wonderful of all in this great story is not the determination and resolve of Mark, nor the sympathy and kindness of Peter, nor the forgiveness of Paul, but the love and the grace of God. It was the love of God, God's beautiful forgiveness, that brought Mark back from failure and sin to the place of usefulness and honor. Oh, the depth of the riches of the love of God!

We are all conscious from time to time of failure. Some may recall deep and tragic failure. You failed yourself, your best self, you failed your friends, you failed as a father, as a husband, as a son or daughter or wife. And some too—and alas, how many such failures there are—

must remember how they have failed Christ, how they have failed as Christians. If so, remember the story of Mark and take heart again! The deserter, the quitter and the coward, one of the worst failures in the history of the Bible, passes from the stage of New Testament history in the golden light of that last and great message of Paul: "Take Mark, and bring him with thee: for he is profitable to me for the ministry."

IX

MICAIAH—IN PRISON FOR CONSCIENCE' SAKE

> "There is yet one man, . . . but I hate him."
>
> I KINGS 22:8

WE ALL HAVE THAT "ONE MAN" WITHIN OUR BREAST, and the natural man hates him, just as Ahab, the king of Israel, hated Micaiah, the fearless prophet of the Lord.

Jehoshaphat, the good king of Judah, had gone down to visit Ahab, the wicked king of Israel, at Samaria. Ahab gave him a great reception and banquet and killed sheep and oxen for him in abundance and for the people that were with him. At this banquet Ahab proposed to Jehoshaphat that they go up and attack the stronghold of Ramoth-gilead, which was still occupied by their inveterate enemies the Syrians. Flattered with the honors paid him by Ahab, Jehoshaphat, whose inclinations generally were Godward, but who on more than one occasion was led astray by wrong associations, said to Ahab that he would go with him on this expedition: "I am as thou art, my people as thy people, my horses as thy horses." In other words, Jehoshaphat pledged all the resources of his kingdom to this war against Ramoth-gilead and Syria.

But Jehoshaphat, who was a godly man, did not wish to start upon such an expedition without first inquiring of the Lord. So he said to Ahab, "Enquire, I pray thee, at the word of the Lord." In answer to this the king of Israel gathered together four hundred of his prophets, or so-called prophets, all of whom made it their business, not to declare the word of the Lord, but to tell Ahab to do whatever he wanted to do. These four hundred prophets appeared in the throne room of Ahab's ivory palace at Samaria. The two kings were seated on two thrones, each one of them resplendent with his crown upon his head and crimson and purple robes upon his body. The king of Israel then inquired of the four hundred, saying, "Shall I go against Ramoth-gilead to battle, or shall I forbear?" With one voice these false prophets said, "Go up; for the Lord shall deliver it into the hand of the king."

Jehoshaphat, the king of Judah, apparently was a little disturbed at this quick shout of unanimous approval. He probably did not like the looks of these false prophets. So he said to the king of Israel, "Is there not here a prophet of the Lord besides, that we might enquire of him?" Ahab answered: "There is yet one man, Micaiah the son of Imlah, by whom we may enquire of the Lord: but I hate him; for he doth not prophesy good concerning me, but evil." But Jehoshaphat insisted that this prophet of the Lord be called in. A messenger was then dispatched to summon Micaiah.

In the meantime one of the false prophets, Zedekiah, put on a bit of acting or show to impress Ahab. He fastened horns of iron on his head and, appearing before the thrones of the two kings, said: "Thus saith the Lord, With these shalt thou push the Syrians, until thou have consumed them." Then all the four hundred shouted together: "Go up to Ramoth-gilead, and prosper: for the Lord shall deliver it into the king's hand."

When the messenger arrived at the house of Micaiah to summon him before the kings, he said to him in effect: "All the other prophets, the four hundred, have told Ahab that if he goes up against Ramoth-gilead he will be victorious. As a friend I would advise you, when you appear before the king, to say the same thing." But this messenger knew not with whom he was speaking, for Micaiah answered immediately: "As the Lord liveth, what the Lord saith unto me, that will I speak."

Micaiah was brought before Ahab and Jehoshaphat. There he stood, one against four hundred. The two kings, resplendent in their robes and diadems, looked down upon him. Zedekiah, with the iron horns in his hands, stood near, looking scornfully upon Micaiah, and in the great hall the four hundred were silent as they waited to see what Micaiah would say.

Then Ahab addressed the fearless prophet and said: "Shall we go against Ramoth-gilead to battle, or shall we forbear?"

Micaiah answered: "Go, and prosper: for the Lord shall deliver it into the hand of the king." He was speaking, of course, ironically. Ahab's conscience let him know at once that God did not approve the expedition against Ramoth-gilead. As Elijah mocked and defied the false prophets of this same king, so Micaiah mocked them by telling Ahab to go up against Ramoth-gilead and prosper.

The angry king, seeing that Micaiah was mocking him, said to the prophet: "How many times shall I adjure thee that thou tell me nothing but that which is true in the name of the Lord?"

Then Micaiah told him the truth. He gave it in the form of a vision: "I saw all Israel scattered upon the hills, as sheep that have not a shepherd: and the Lord said, These have no master: let them return every man to his house in peace." This vision was a prediction of the defeat and overthrow of Israel in the coming battle, and the calamity which would come upon the nation because it would have no shepherd and king.

Angry and out of sorts, the King of Israel exclaimed to Jehoshaphat: "Did I not tell thee that he would prophesy no good concerning me?" Then Micaiah continued his speech and told of another vision. At a conclave in heaven, with all the host of heaven present, God asked: "Who shall persuade Ahab, that he may go up and fall at Ramoth-gilead?" One suggested this plan and one suggested another plan. Then there came forth a spirit and stood before the Lord and said, "I will persuade him." And God said, "Wherewith?" The spirit answered: "I will go forth, and I will be a lying spirit in the mouth of all his prophets." Micaiah said to Ahab: "The Lord hath put a lying spirit in the mouth of all these thy prophets, and the Lord hath spoken evil concerning thee."

That was a magnificent stand for conscience and truth that Micaiah made, one against four hundred. The immediate consequence was that he was smitten in the face by the leader of the false prophets, Zedekiah, and cast into prison by the king, who told the jailer to "feed him with bread of affliction and with water of affliction." But the name of Micaiah lives forever because of his fidelity to conscience and the word of God.

TWO TRUTHS ABOUT CONSCIENCE

There are two great truths about conscience which are brought out in this stirring narrative. The first is that, as Luther said at the Diet of Worms, when he was asked to recant and deny what he had written and taught in his books, "It is neither safe nor wise to do anything against conscience." Ahab found that out. He was always fighting against his conscience, and always his conscience was overcoming him. When he met Elijah at the time of the great drought that had come down upon Israel because of the king's wickedness, he cried out: "Hast thou found me, O mine enemy?" Elijah, as the incarnation of Conscience, had indeed found him. Here Ahab called conscience, in the person of the fearless and incorruptible Micaiah, his enemy. When Jehoshaphat asked if there was not yet a prophet of the Lord of whom they could inquire, Ahab answered: "There is yet one man, . . . but I hate him." Conscience always stands in the way of Ramoth-gilead expeditions. Four hundred voices may tell you to go forward and do what you want to do, and only one voice will say to you not to go, that the expedition will end in disaster and judgment and death.

That was what happened to Ahab. He heeded the voice of the four hundred false prophets and cast the one true prophet into prison. So men cast their conscience into prison. He summoned his captains and his army, and together with Jehoshaphat, who probably was somewhat reluctant to go, marched up against Ramoth-gilead. In the great battle which followed, Ahab, when he heard the blare of the trumpets and saw the sun flashing on the helmets and shields and chariots of the Syrian host, remembered very clearly the word of Micaiah warning him not to go. Now the voice of conscience was speaking louder than all those four hundred false prophets. Ahab thought that perhaps he could escape death in the battle by disguising himself as a private soldier. This he did, putting off his royal robes and wearing the armor of a common soldier. But there is no disguise which judgment and retribution cannot penetrate. Jehoshaphat, however, was wearing his royal robes. The king of Syria had commanded his captains to fight neither with small nor great, save only with the king of Israel. Ahab was the man he wanted to kill. At first the captains pursued Jehoshaphat in his chariot, still wearing his royal robes, thinking he was Ahab. But when they learned that he was the king of Judah and not the king of Israel, they turned back from pursuing him.

It looked as if in the rout of the battle Ahab was going to escape. But no! A certain man drew a bow at a venture. The hand of God was on that bow. "A certain man drew a bow at a venture, and smote the king of Israel between the joints of the harness." Until the sun went down Ahab was stayed up in his chariot against the Syrians, but at the evening he died. His chariot was then driven back to Samaria. Some of his officers took the chariot down to the pool of Samaria to wash out the blood that had stained it, and as they did so the dogs came and licked up his blood, the very dogs which had licked up the blood of Naboth, whom Ahab had slain that he might take his vineyard, thus fulfilling the prophecy of Elijah: "In the place where dogs licked the blood of Naboth shall dogs lick thy blood, even thine." No, it is never safe and never wise to do anything against conscience. In the end, conscience is the victor and the judge.

THE GRANDEUR OF OBEYING CONSCIENCE

If Ahab's history and death show the folly of disobeying and wronging conscience, the history of Micaiah shows the grandeur of obedience to conscience. In the witness that he made to God and the truth Micaiah was faithful to conscience and the word of God in spite of the majority, the four hundred, who gave a different counsel to the king. He was faithful to conscience in spite of the insults and ridicule which were heaped upon him. He was faithful to conscience although it meant the loss of preferment at the court. He was faithful to conscience although it meant the darkness of the dungeon. But in the dungeon he had that lamp and candle which no wind of evil or human tyranny can ever extinguish—the answer of a good conscience.

When Hugh Latimer, the great reformer of the sixteenth century in England, was preaching one day before Henry VIII, he offended the king by some plain speaking in his sermon. The king ordered him to preach again the next Sunday and to make apology for the offense he had given. On the next Sunday, after he had given out his text, Latimer began by addressing his own soul: "Hugh Latimer, dost thou know before whom thou art this day to speak? To the high and mighty monarch, the king's most excellent majesty, who can take away thy life if thou offendest. Therefore take heed that thou speakest not a word that may displease. But then, consider well, Hugh. Dost thou not know from whence thou comest, upon whose message thou art sent? Even by the great and mighty God, who is all present, and who beholdest all thy ways, and who is able to cast thy soul into hell? Therefore take care that thou deliverest thy message faithfully." He then repeated the sermon he had preached to the king the Sunday before. All the court were full of expectation to know what the fate of this bold preacher would be. That night the king summoned him, and, in a stern voice, asked him how he could be so bold as to preach to the king in that manner. Latimer replied that he had merely discharged his duty and obeyed his conscience. Upon which the king arose from his seat and, taking the good man by the hand, embraced him saying: "Blessed be God I have so honest a servant." This was the same Latimer who was burned at the stake at Smithfield in the reign of Bloody Mary. In his dying hour he tasted the victory, the thrill of moral victory, for he greeted his fellow martyr Ridley with the famous words: "Be of good comfort, Master Ridley, and play the man. We shall this day light such a candle, by God's grace, in England, as I trust shall never be put out!"

By the heroic and lonely stand which he took, Micaiah takes rank with the kings and princes of the moral world —With Joseph, who said to the temptress, "How then can I do this great wickedness, and sin against God?" With Daniel, who opened his window toward Jerusalem and prayed to God, though he was cast into the lions' den for it. With John the Baptist, who rebuked Herod and Herodias for their sin. In the end, what looks like a lonely minority is always the majority. When Ahab was slain in the battle against which the prophet warned him, and all Israel was scattered like sheep without a shepherd in the hill, where then were the four hundred false prophets?

There are students of our national life today who declare that the United States is in a moral decline, comparable to that which engulfed the Roman Empire. One of these observers says: "Everything is covered with dirt because the world has lost its morals." What we need above all else is a revival of Christian conscience, and of courage to testify to Christian standards in the court of a hostile world. When he was in the Tower of London, William Penn said: "My prison shall be my grave before I will budge a jot, for I owe my conscience to no mortal man." And John Bunyan, in Bedford Jail, when offered release if he would promise to cease preaching, said: "Moss shall grow on these eyebrows before I surrender my principles or violate my conscience." It was that loyalty to conscience which qualified Bunyan to write that great tribute to conscience, when he told of the passing of Mr. Honest:

When the day that he was to be gone was come, he addressed himself to go over the river. Now, the river at that time overflowed its banks in some places; but Mr. Honest in his lifetime had spoken to one Good-conscience to meet him there; the which also he did, and lent him his hand, and so helped him over.

X

PHILIP—THE MAN WHO MADE
A CITY GLAD

> "We entered into the house of Philip
> the evangelist."
>
> ACTS 21:8

WHEN WE SPEAK OF JOHN OR PETER WE SAY "THE
Apostle John," "the Apostle Peter," but when we speak of
Paul we almost always say "Paul the apostle," as if he
were, and indeed in many respects he was, the pre-eminent
one among all the apostles of the Lord. Likewise when we
speak of Philip we do not say "the Evangelist Philip," but
always, as the book of Acts names him, "Philip the evangelist." He stands at the head of all the evangelists, not
only because he is the first so named, but because of what
he was and what he did in the name of Christ.

Philip the evangelist is not to be confused with the
other Philip, who is one of the twelve apostles. This Philip
was one of the Seven who were chosen by the Christian
disciples at Jerusalem to administer the charities of the
Church. The Church at the very beginning felt its obliga-
tion to the poor and needy; but as usual there were com-
plainers and faultfinders. Some of the Christians of Greek
blood and background complained that their widows and
other needy ones were discriminated against in the dis-
tribution of alms in favor of the needy who were Jewish-
Christians. The apostles felt that they could not turn
aside from their special ministry of preaching and prayer

[108]

to look after this matter, and therefore they instructed the disciples at Jerusalem to select seven men of good report to administer the charity of the Church. They are often spoken of as deacons, but that name is not given to them in the book of Acts. Two of the Seven achieved an immortality of fame—Stephen, the first martyr, and Philip the evangelist.

After the death of Stephen a fierce persecution broke out against the Christians at Jerusalem, and the chief persecutor was Saul of Tarsus, who had held the garments of those who had stoned Stephen. Great numbers of the believers at Jerusalem fled the city, although the apostles themselves remained at Jerusalem. Those who fled the city "went every where preaching the word." And thus God made the wrath of man to praise him. The fierce persecution which was led by Paul, then called Saul, was intended to root out and destroy Christianity. Instead of that it spread it throughout that part of the world. It was an early illustration of what the subsequent ages demonstrated so often, that, as the fiery Tertullian phrased it, "The blood of the martyrs is the seed of the Church." Some of those who were driven out of Jerusalem went to the island of Cyprus, some to Antioch. Some of the Jews who were converted at Cyprus came to Antioch and preached to the Greeks there. That was the beginning of the Church at Antioch, and where the disciples were "called Christians first."

PHILIP AT SAMARIA

When he fled from Jerusalem Philip the evangelist went down to Samaria and preached the gospel there. That sounds to us a very natural and ordinary thing. But it was an amazing and extraordinary fact, and is a demonstration of the power of the gospel to break down the walls of alienation and caste and hatred and contempt. Paul declared that Christ had abolished the three castes which divided and burdened mankind in that day: the caste of sex, the caste of condition, and the caste of religion and race. He said: "There is neither Jew nor Greek, . . . bond nor free, . . . male nor female: for ye all are one in Christ Jesus." The preaching of the gospel to the people of Samaria is the earliest example that we have of the breaking down of the wall of caste and prejudice.

The Samaritans were a mixture of Jews from the northern Kingdom of Israel and heathen from Babylon, who had been brought in to settle the land by Sargon when Samaria was captured and her people carried into captivity. They had some expectation of the Messiah and some sacred rites and rituals of their own, and a temple on Mount Gerizim. But they were looked upon with the utmost contempt by the Jews. When the temple was rebuilt in the time of Zerubbabel, they were excluded from having any part in its restoration. We get some idea of how the Jews looked upon them when we remember that in his great parable of the man who went down to Jericho and fell among thieves, and which tells how the priest and Levite "passed by on the other side," and how a third traveler came along and ministered to the man, set him upon his beast and carried him to an inn, Jesus made a point of noting that the third traveler was "a certain Samaritan," that is, the last person in the world to whom a Jew would have attributed any of the virtues of religion and humanity. And when Jesus himself talked with the woman at the well of Samaria, that five-times married woman of unsavory reputation, the woman wondered that he would talk with her, and said: "How is it that thou, being a Jew, askest drink of me, who am a woman of Samaria?"

This gives you some idea of how completely Christ had won the heart of Philip when you hear of Philip going down into Samaria and preaching Christ unto them. He did this so earnestly and so successfully that there was great joy in that city. Unclean spirits were cast out, the sick were healed, and those who sorrowed rejoiced. "There was great joy in that city."

That was a prophecy of what the gospel can do, and often has done, wherever it has been truly preached and truly believed and truly practiced. It has the power to cast out evil spirits. There is no doubt that when the gospel speaks of evil spirit being cast out, that is exactly what it means. It is not a figure of speech but a reference to those spirits of evil which Christ himself on different occasions commanded to come out of the hearts and bodies of men. I have heard missionaries of the cross relate experiences in heathen lands which left no doubt in their minds as to the active agency of evil spirits. What evil spirits do under the leadership of their prince, the Evil One himself, from whose power Christ taught us in the Lord's Prayer to ask to be delivered, about that at least there can be no doubt. There are the evil spirits that manifest their work in greed, malice, pride, anger, cruelty, licentiousness, and blasphemy. Time and time again those evil spirits have been cast out. The evil spirit of blasphemy was cast out of no less a person than Paul the apostle himself. No wonder there was joy in that city. Wherever men turn from the wrong way to the right way, and from the power of Satan unto the power of God, there will be joy. Crossing the Atlantic once with the English poet laureate John Masefield, I told him that sometimes when preaching on repentance I quoted from his *Everlasting Mercy,* one of the greatest things on repentance ever written, where he tells of the great joy that swept over that drunken, licentious, vile man Saul Kane, when he had been converted and turned to God.

> O glory of the lighted mind.
> How dead I'd been, how dumb, how blind.
> The station brook, to my new eyes,
> Was babbling out of Paradise,
> The waters rushing from the rain
> Were singing Christ has risen again.
> I thought all earthly creatures knelt
> From rapture of the joy I felt.
> The narrow station-wall's brick ledge,
> The wild hop withering in the hedge,
> The lights in huntsman's upper storey
> Were parts of an eternal glory,
> Were God's eternal garden flowers.
> I stood in bliss at this for hours.[1]

PHILIP AND THE ETHIOPIAN

It must have seemed strange to Philip when he received the intimation through the angel of the Lord that he was to leave populous Samaria, where he had won such eminent success as a preacher of the gospel, and where he had brought joy to so many people, and go down into the desert country to the south about Gaza. But Philip was always the man who obeyed the word of the Lord. He effaced himself completely. Leaving Samaria to the ministry of John and Peter, who had heard of his work, and had come down to Samaria to carry it on, he took the road to the far south.

[1] Copyright 1911 by the author; used by permission of The Macmillan Company, publishers.

At length he came to the place where the road on which he was traveling from Samaria joined the road coming from Jerusalem. As he was walking along this road, no doubt troubled in his mind as to just what God meant to do with him there, he saw coming along near him a considerable caravan, in the midst of which was an Ethiopian, the treasurer of Queen Candace of Ethiopia. This distinguished man was returning from a visit to Jerusalem. There is no doubt that the purpose of the visit was not political or financial but religious. And when we say that, we must remember that this Ethiopian had traveled over twelve hundred miles from far down below Egypt to worship at Jerusalem, probably as a proselyte at the Gate. In making that journey he had passed through the land that was pre-eminently the land of religion, the land of colossal temples and pyramids, the land of tombs, the land where the science of life beyond the grave had been developed to a most extraordinary degree. Yet this finance minister of Ethiopia passed all that by and made his way to Jerusalem. Now he is on his way back, and he has in his possession a copy of the Scriptures, the Old Testament.

We wonder how he came to know of the Scriptures and of the worship of Jehovah. Did some far-traveling Jewish merchant, penetrating far-off Ethiopia, bring the knowledge of the true God, of the Old Testament, to him? The Ethiopians, of course, claim that the Queen of Sheba was one of their queens; that she had a son named Menelik by Solomon, and that that was the link between Ethiopia and the Jews. That name Menelik has persisted in Ethiopia's dynasty almost down to our own day. But however it was accomplished, this man had learned of Moses and the Scriptures of the Old Testament.

At the direction of the Holy Spirit, Philip drew near to this chariot, with its Arabian steeds and its regal decorations. The Ethiopian was reading from the prophecy of Isaiah, and, as most people still do in Eastern lands, he was reading aloud. You can go into some of the mosques over there, and some of their schools and colleges, and hear the murmur of voices as they read aloud. That was what this Ethiopian treasurer was doing.

Philip probably caught a few words as the Ethiopian scanned the page; at least enough to let him know that he was reading from Isaiah. So he said to him: "Understandest thou what thou readest?" That to us has something of a note of abruptness, almost impertinence. How would you and I like it if someone saw us reading a book or a newspaper and came over and asked us if we understood what we were reading? But here it is plain from what followed that there was no note of discourtesy or impudence in the way Philip asked the question, for the Ethiopian at once said: "How can I, except some man should guide me?" "And he desired Philip that he would come up and sit with him." That is the first step if a man is going to come to Christ—humility. "The humble shall see this, and be glad." The reason many stay away from Christ, and the reason many already within the Church practically deny the gospel of Christ, is because they lack that humility which Jesus said was necessary: "Except ye be converted, and become as little children, ye shall not enter into the kingdom of heaven."

The Ethiopian desired that Philip would come up and sit beside him. "Come up here alongside of me," he said in effect, "and explain to me, if you will, this passage which I have been reading." At a command from his master, the slave who was driving pulled up his team, and

Philip stepped into the chariot and sat down beside the Ethiopian.

The particular place in Isaiah where the man was reading was one of the great and sublime passages in all the Bible, the fifty-third chapter: "Who hath believed our report? And to whom is the arm of the Lord revealed? . . . He was wounded for our transgressions, he was bruised for our iniquities: the chastisement of our peace was upon him; and with his stripes we are healed." The particular verse which the Ethiopian had come to was this: "He is brought as a lamb to the slaughter, and as a sheep before her shearers is dumb, so he openeth not his mouth. He was taken from prison and from judgment: and who shall declare his generation?"

Pointing to those words and repeating them to Philip, the Ethiopian said to him: "I pray thee, of whom speaketh the prophet this? Of himself, or of some other man?" He was asking: "Does Isaiah mean that he himself was led as a lamb to the slaughter, and that he opened not his mouth before his accusers? Or does he refer to some other man?"

"Then Philip opened his mouth, and began at the same scripture, and preached unto him Jesus." At Samaria, when he preached to the hundreds, he preached unto them Christ; and here, when he preached to only one man, it is the same sermon; he "preached unto him Jesus." This is one of those great lost sermons which we would give a good deal to recover. What would we not give if we could have that sermon which Jesus preached to those two on the way to Emmaus on the evening of the Resurrection Day, when, "beginning at Moses and all the prophets, he expounded unto them in all the scriptures the things concerning himself." What a wealth of light that would throw upon the pages of the Old Testament! And what

[115]

would we not give to have that sermon which Philip preached that day to the Ethiopian as the chariot rolled slowly along southward, and when he took for his text the fifty-third chapter of Isaiah! But because that was his text we can certainly reproduce, in substance at least, what Philip must have told the Ethiopian. He preached to him Jesus as the Son of God, and yet one who was despised and rejected of men, a man of sorrows and acquainted with grief; who bore our griefs and carried our sorrows; who was wounded for our transgressions; oppressed and afflicted; cut off out of the land of the living, numbered with the transgressors, and put to death upon the cross; but who rose again from the dead; who shall see of the travail of his soul and be satisfied; who welcomes into his Kingdom all those who repent and believe. Some modern preachers by-pass this great chapter, or give it some strange fantastic meaning and substitute for Christ the "people of Israel." But not so Philip when he preached on it; and not so Jesus himself, for in the same night in which he was betrayed Jesus himself took up this chapter, this great portrait of himself, and quoting the words "He was numbered with the transgressors," said that this prophecy was now to be fulfilled in him.

Philip did not preach Jesus to the Ethiopian as only another in the great line of the Hebrew prophets; he did not present him as a saintly character; he did not proclaim him as a great thinker, as the founder of a new school of thought, or as a great moral and social reformer; but he preached him and proclaimed him as the suffering, dying, and atoning Son of God. That is the Christ of Isaiah. It is the Christ of the apostles, the Christ of the prophets, the Christ of the martyrs, the Christ of the redeemed in heaven, the Christ of the ages, the Christ who is able to save unto the uttermost them that come unto him, and fill their hearts with joy.

Now let us look at the results of this sermon. As Philip preached to the Ethiopian, the Spirit opened his heart. God's greatest miracle, the miracle of repentance and faith, was wrought in the Ethiopian's heart. He believed in Jesus, and he wanted to become his follower and trust in his salvation. As they were rolling along in the chariot they came to a pool of water. When he saw it, the Ethiopian said to Philip: "See, here is water; what doth hinder me to be baptized?" But Philip, although pleased, no doubt, to win so notable a convert from so far distant a land, was careful to make sure that the man was a real believer, so he said to him: "If thou believest with all thine heart, thou mayest." The Ethiopian answered and said: "I believe that Jesus Christ is the Son of God." Then the chariot was stopped and the two went down into the water, and the Ethiopian was baptized by Philip into the name of the Father and of the Son and of the Holy Ghost.

There they parted, the preacher and his convert. Philip went on his way till he came to Caesarea. The Ethiopian rolled on southward in his chariot. He "went on his way," we are told, "rejoicing." When Philip preached to the hundreds in Samaria there was great joy in that city; likewise when he preached to this one man who repented and believed and was baptized, he "went on his way rejoicing." In that dark and cruel kingdom of Ethiopia, we doubt not, he witnessed faithfully to the Saviour whom Philip had preached unto him and in whose redeeming blood he had come to trust. The psalmist, ages before, had prophesied and predicted: "Ethiopia shall soon stretch out her hands unto God." Now that prophecy was wonderfully fulfilled.

[117]

PHILIP AND PAUL

The third episode in the life and ministry of Philip came long after this one of which we have just been speaking, probably twenty years later. Philip was living at Caeserea, on the coast. He commanded his children after him, for he has four virgin daughters who have given themselves to the work of the Lord, and who prophesy and speak in the name of the Lord. Now Paul, on his last journey up to Jerusalem, not knowing the things that were going to befall him there, save that the Holy Spirit witnessed, saying that bonds and affliction were waiting for him, coming clear from Greece through Macedonia, over to Troas, and down the coast of Asia Minor to the island of Rhodes, and then to Cyprus, landed at Tyre, and after a few days came to Caesarea. There he went to the home of Philip the evangelist and was his guest for "many days."

Paul tells us how he once, early in his ministry, spent fifteen days with Peter. That must have been a wonderful fifteen days, and we can well imagine what Peter and Paul talked about, and what exchange of experiences they had, and what exchange of hope too. I wish we could have been in that home there by the seaside at Caesarea and listened to the conversation of Philip and Paul, with those four devout daughters ministering to them and listening eagerly to their conversation.

We wonder what they talked about. Philip, no doubt, told Paul about his election as one of the Seven, and how, at the time of the persecution, which Paul himself had led (although Philip probably did not mention that fact), he left the city and came down to Samaria, where he preached Christ unto them, and how there was great joy in the city. And then how he preached Christ to the Ethiopian, the treasurer of Queen Candace, and brought him into the Kingdom of God, and sent him on his way rejoicing. And what a story Paul had to tell to Philip! His early days at Tarsus; how he sat at the feet of Gamaliel in Jerusalem; how he held the clothes of them that stoned Stephen; and how he heard Stephen pray for those who stoned him; his conversion at the gate of Damascus; his preaching at Antioch; and all the missionary journeys; his imprisonments and scourgings and stonings and shipwrecks; and how it had been made clear to him that still more trials and sufferings for the sake of Christ awaited him. But what was that, he would say to Philip, compared with the joy of serving him who loved him and gave himself for him!

When I read in the New Testament of Paul spending fifteen days with Peter, and many days there at Caesarea with Philip, it makes me wonder about the joys of heaven. No doubt that will be one of the chief joys for those who love Christ and love one another—to talk together. Socrates said he looked forward with a thrill of expectation to conversing with Homer and the mighty dead of the ancient world. If even a pagan could say that, then how much more the Christian believer can look forward with expectation to conversing with the mighty dead of the Bible and of Christian history. Think of having a talk with Abraham, with Joseph, with Moses, and Samuel and Isaiah, and most of all, for me at least, with David. And among those of the New Testament, with Peter and John and Mary of Magdala and the penitent thief, and with Philip and Stephen and Paul himself! When Philip and Paul talked together there on the seashore at Caesarea, that was, it seems to me, a picture, a preview, as it were, of the final communion of the saints in heaven.

[119]

So in that sweet and pleasant converse Philip the evangelist passes from our view but not from our memory. His story tells us, first of all, what a layman can do for Christ. Philip was not an apostle nor an ordained minister. He was chosen to do a work of charity for the Church. But he rose far above that social service and made himself a great winner of souls. That today is the greatest need of the Church, that its lay members should work and witness for Christ and give gladly and freely of their time, of their strength, of their talents, their money, and their enthusiasm.

Again, the story of Philip tells us what the gospel is, what the message of the true preacher must ever be. To the people of Samaria, then to the Ethiopian chancellor in the chariot, Philip preached Christ. He preached the two great facts about Christ, which together make up our Christian faith: first, that he is the Son of God; and second, that he gave himself and died for our sins upon the cross. He shows too what it is to become a Christian. It is to believe with all our heart and confess with our mouth those great truths, and take them for the need of our own souls, and then to unite with the Christian fellowship, the Christian community, the Christian Church. That is what Philip did. When he confessed his faith he was baptized and received into the Church.

And last of all, Philip strikes the ever-resounding chord of joy. There was great joy in the city of Samaria when he preached Christ there; and when he preached Christ to the Ethiopian eunuch, he went on his way rejoicing. Do you know that joy? Amid all the mists and mirages and illusions and transiencies of time, do you know the satisfaction, the joy, of standing upon the unshaken and eternal rock, Jesus Christ, the same yesterday, today and forever?

XI

ANTIPAS—A FAITHFUL MARTYR

"Antipas, . . . my faithful martyr, who
was slain among you, where Satan
dwelleth."

REV. 2:13

THIS IS THE GREATEST EPITAPH OF THE BIBLE. IN THE
days of his flesh Christ promised eternal life and eternal
reward to those who are faithful to him. If they confess
his name before the world, he will confess their names
before his Father in heaven. But here Christ, speaking to
John on Patmos, singles out and names one man as having
been faithful unto death, and that one man is Antipas,
his faithful witness, who died for Christ at Pergamos.

Pergamos was one of the cities of the Seven Churches
to which Christ sent his message through John. It is located some seventy miles north of Smyrna, and on the
highway which led across that part of Asia Minor from
Philadelphia to Sardis, to Thyatira, and on to Troas. The
ruins at Pergamos are the most imposing of any of the
cities of the Seven Churches. Following the ancient road
which winds up the mountain side to the Acropolis, and
where the ruts worn in the stones of the road by the chariot
wheels are clearly visible, one reaches the pleateau on the
top of the mount. The plain is strewn with the ruins of
palaces, temples, amphitheaters, forums, and market
places. Pergamos was the center of the worship of the god
of healing, Aesculapius. This god was worshiped under
the symbol of the serpent, and one was kept there in his

temple. There too was the famous altar of Zeus, on the base of which were depicted the battles between the giants and the gods. There too, when Pergamos was in its glory, one might have seen the famous sculpture "The Dying Galatian," celebrating the victory of the king of Pergamos over the Galatians or the Gauls. "The Dying Gladiator," or "Dying Gaul," in the Capitoline Museum at Rome, and so familiar to thousands of travelers, is a copy of the original statue on the walls of Pergamos. In Pergamos too was one of the world's greatest libraries. It was from this library that Mark Antony, to please Cleopatra, transported the parchments or books to Alexandria, to be added to the collection of that famous library. Pergamos was a city of power, of Roman authority, and also a place of great iniquity, so much so that Christ said to the church at Pergamos: "I know . . . where thou dwellest, even where Satan's seat is." Every great city is in a certain sense a seat of Satan; for the great cities, then in the days of Pergamos, and today, where thousands and millions of people are flung together, afford Satan the best theater for the display of his infernal power. There, more than anywhere else, we behold the terrible havoc and ruin wrought by sin in the lives of men.

But in the midst of this wicked city there was a Christian church. Who established the church? We do not know. Paul himself may have stopped there on one of his journeys across Asia Minor. More likely, John, who lived at Ephesus, or one of John's assistants, first preached the gospel in this seat of Satan. Had you and I been there on one of those bright, unclouded days, we might have seen multitudes flocking to the amphitheater to view the bloody spectacles of the arena; and others thronging the temple of Venus with its licentious rites; and others going to the baths by the temple of Aesculapius, where the serpent was worshiped. But here are a few men and women, no doubt not many wise, or great, or noble among them, as Paul says, who are going to this upper chamber in one of the houses in a poor section of the city, or who are meeting in a cave halfway down the mountain, back of the theater, toward the river Caicus. There they worship the Lamb of God. In his message to this church Christ says: "I know thy works, and where thou dwellest." He praises it for holding fast his Name, and for not denying his faith, even in the terrible days of persecution, "wherein Antipas was my faithful martyr, who was slain among you."

THE CONVERSION OF ANTIPAS

This is all that we hear of Antipas. But this one mention opens a door of rich thought and imagination. Since he has this Greek name, we shall assume that he was a man of education and scholarship, perhaps the custodian or librarian of that great library at Pergamos, where he handles and cherishes the vast store of manuscripts which record the learning and the history of the ancient world. One evening, on his way home from the library to his villa on the banks of the Caicus, he sees a group of plain-looking people standing in the shadow of one of the temples. A man is addressing them in earnest speech. Antipas pauses to listen. His ear catches words that are new to him, and which, as a scholar, arouse his interest: "regeneration," "atonement," "justification," "salvation," and every now and then the name "Jesus," and "Christ." The next night he stops again and listens to the same speaker, and then hears them sing one of their hymns. The seed of truth, the Word of God, finds lodgment in his heart, and in the end Antipas becomes a follower of the Lamb of God, a man destined to be mentioned nineteen hundred years afterward in other Christian churches, and in a part of the world not then known to be in existence, as one who, among the great multitude who have followed Christ, was singled out by Christ himself and named as his faithful martyr and disciple.

Although this is all we hear of Antipas, we can be certain of certain facts about him.

ANTIPAS WAS A BELIEVER IN CHRIST

Pergamos, as we have seen, was a city of intense wickedness, steeped in idolatry and licentiousness, a veritable seat of Satan; and yet in this satanic environment here is a man who leads a true and beautiful Christian life. Horace Walpole, commenting on the character of Lord Somers, one of the friends of John Locke, the philosopher, said of him: "He was one of those divine men who, like a chapel in a palace, remain unprofaned, while all the rest is tyranny, corruption, and folly." So was Antipas at Pergamos. This world has never been, and is not now, a friend of the Christian life; and yet, in spite of that, in every age there have been those whom Christ could commend. In Paul's letter to the Philippians, written when he was a prisoner at Rome, and evidently at the Praetorium, or military headquarters of Nero, you come upon this stirring salutation, "All the saints salute you; chiefly they that are of Caesar's household." The saints of Caesar's household! And who was that Caesar? None other than the wicked Nero, matricide, fratricide, burner of the Christians, and at length an ignoble suicide. His household, or palace, was a very cesspool of corruption and immorality; and yet in that very household, and in such an atmosphere as that, there were true followers of Christ whose

[124]

greetings Paul sends to believers at Philippi. When you feel that your surroundings, perhaps your home, perhaps the office or the shop where you work, the soldiers in your barracks or mess hall, perhaps the company into which of necessity you are thrown, when you feel that all this is unfavorable for the cultivation of the Christian life, remember those saints of Caesar's household. Remember Antipas, the faithful witness of Christ, there at the very seat of Satan. I have seen exquisite and beautiful flowers growing on the border of an ugly and ill-smelling swamp. That is the wonderful thing about the Christian life. It can spring up and reveal its beauty and shed its fragrance under every condition and circumstance.

ANTIPAS WAS FAITHFUL IN SPITE OF WORLDLY LOSS

One day perhaps the prefect, or consul, at Pergamos called him before him and said, "Antipas, what is this I hear about you running around with those wretched people of 'The Way,' those miserable Christians?"

"It is true," answers Antipas. "I am a Christian."

"But do you not know," says the consul, "that they are under suspicion, that they are charged with being in conspiracy against the empire? That they practice secret abominations in their night meetings?"

"Yes," says Antipas, "I know that charge has been made; but, sir, it is not true. I have found them to be law-abiding, hard-working, faithful and honorable men and women."

"Well," says the consul, "whether it is true or not, Antipas, you cannot hold the important post of librarian in this, almost the most famous library of the world, and at the same time run around with those Christians. You will have to choose, Antipas, between this post with all its honor

[125]

and distinction, and the fine living which it gives you, and these Christians and your Christ, as you call him."

"I have chosen," says Antipas. "I will be faithful to Christ."

Dismissed from his post, and with a family dependent upon him, Antipas faces the world anew. Perhaps, although altogether unaccustomed to manual labor, he gets a job in the market place, or with the gangs of men repairing the Roman highway that ran from Pergamos to Troas. His loyalty to Christ has cost him something. The religion of Christ has so changed the world that in many parts of the world no one will suffer loss because of the fact that he is a Christian; and yet even in the Christian part of the world there are things that the true Christian will not do. There are customs to which he will not bow; and because he will not, he will still suffer loss.

ANTIPAS WAS A CHRISTIAN AT SATAN'S SEAT

Sometimes I think that more people are laughed and scorned and ridiculed out of their faith than are frightened out of it by persecution. It will often require more courage to be pointed out as peculiar, as old fashioned, and strait laced, than it does to face physical violence and persecution. It is written of Moses, in that great roll call of the heroes of the faith, that he chose to "suffer affliction with the people of God, than to enjoy the pleasures of sin for a season; esteeming the reproach of Christ greater riches than the treasures in Egypt." Would that we could all do that, esteem the reproach and ridicule for the sake of Christ not a sad and unfortunate and lamentable thing, but true riches, greater riches, than the world can offer us!

There is a fine passage in *Tom Brown's School Days* which tells of a boy who had the courage to stand up

[126]

against ridicule. A new boy had come to the school, and on his first night, in a room where there were twelve beds and boys, he knelt down to say his prayers. Tom Brown's head was turned just in time to see a heavy slipper flying through the air at the head of the kneeling boy. When the lights went out a little later Tom Brown thought of his own mother, and the prayers that she had taught him to say, but which he had never said since he came to Rugby. Then and there he made a decision that the next time he went to bed he too would say his prayers. When that next night came the other boys in the room, ready to laugh and scoff at this newcomer who said his prayers, were amazed to see Tom Brown, whom they all respected and feared, kneel down at the side of his bed and pray. That boy's courageous prayer, in spite of ridicule, at length won him the respect of all his companions, and he rose to be one of the most distinguished men of the Church of England.

One night a group of Antipas' friends stopped at his door and said, "Antipas, there is going to be a great show at the Greek theater tonight. Forty thousand people will be there. We are going to raise money to prosecute the war against the savage Galatians. Some of the famous Roman gladiators are going to fight, and there will be dancing and theatrical exhibitions by celebrated beauties and dancers from Rome itself. You can't afford to miss it. Even if you don't care for the show, we are sure that you will go for the sake of patriotism."

But to their surprise Antipas answers, "I cannot go with you. This is the Lord's Day, and even if it were not the Lord's Day, I would not go with you."

"The Lord's Day!" they said, "What is that?"

"It is the day on which my Lord and Saviour rose from the dead for my sins. I am a Christian!"

[127]

"What," they said, "you a Christian! Have you joined that wretched band of slaves, artisans, and released criminals?"

"Yes; I am a Christian!"

"Well," they said, "we will not argue with you longer. When you go to your meeting in that cave with that miserable crowd, you can think of us down at the Greek theater and the great show going on; but there in that cave you will be with that blind beggar, and a couple of the slaves of the prefect, and two or three others."

"Yes;" replied Antipas, "but there is One whom you have forgotten."

"Who is that?"

"He is the Son of God! I shall be in his company."

ANTIPAS WAS A LOYAL CHRISTIAN

Loyalty to Christ sometimes will compel a man to go in lonely places. The crowd, the cheering multitude, will be elsewhere. The whole tide of pagan life at Pergamos was flowing in the opposite direction. Antipas had the courage to tread his path alone. In the Old Testament we have the story of the prophet Micaiah. When the wicked king of Israel, Ahab, invited the king of Judah, Jehoshaphat, to go up with him in battle against Ramoth-gilead, Jehoshaphat wanted first to inquire of the prophets and see what the word of the Lord was. Ahab gathered together his prophets and said to them: "Shall I go against Ramoth-gilead to battle, or shall I forbear?" And the four hundred with one voice said: "Go up; for the Lord will deliver it into the hands of the king." But Jehoshaphat had his doubts about those prophets of Ahab, and wanted to know if there was not a true prophet of the Lord there. The king of Israel said: "There is yet one man . . . by whom we may enquire of the Lord: but I hate him; for he doth not prophesy good concerning me, but evil." His name was Micaiah, the son of Imlah. Micaiah was then brought into the presence of the two kings. Again the four hundred predicted victory in the campaign, declaring that God favored the war. When the king's messenger came to call Micaiah, he told him what the other prophets had said, and warned him that he had better agree with them. But what did Micaiah say? "As the Lord liveth, what the Lord saith unto me, that will I speak." Then Micaiah made his courageous prophecy, in which he disagreed with the four hundred, told them that they were lying prophets, and foretold the defeat of the army and the death of the king of Israel. It was one against four hundred! That is what the world needs, men who are not afraid to stand alone. When the vote on the repeal of the prohibition amendment was being taken in the Michigan legislature, the vote stood ninety-nine for repeal, one against it. When the vote was announced a man in the gallery sprang up and cried out: "God bless that one man who voted No!"

The name of Antipas may be a title more than a name, for it is made up two Greek words which mean "against all." Antipas was the "Withstander of All." He was a man who stood up against the great majority in Pergamos. When the Greek father and theologian Athanasius in the fourth century made his great stand for the deity of Christ against the Arian position, which would have made Christ something less than God, he was told that the world of religious thought was against him. His answer was: "Then it is Athanasius against the world!"

ANTIPAS WAS FAITHFUL IN SPITE OF PERSECUTION

One day one of his old friends on the staff of the library at Pergamos came to him, and secretly in the dead of night, for it was dangerous now to be seen in the company of Christians, and said: "Antipas, while I was resting after the bath at the temple of Aesculapius this afternoon, I heard one of the men say to his companions that you were going to be accused to the prefect as an atheist and as a rebel against Caesar. That, of course, is because they know you are a Christian. I remember your past kindness to me when I worked with you at the library, and I thought I would come and warn you."

Antipas made no change in his habits. When his hard work had ended the next day, and he had his frugal supper, he went again to the cavern on the hillside where the Christians met. They were in the midst of one of their hymns when angry voices were heard outside. Roman soldiers, under the command of a centurion, asked for Antipas. When he rose up to identify himself they seized him and carried him off to the prison cell under the seats of the amphitheater. The next day a great throng assembled. Antipas was led out of his dark cell into the dazzling sunlight of the arena. Two soldiers brought him over to the wall under the canopied seat of the prefect. A clerk read the charge against him: "A Christian, a rebel against Caesar, an atheist who would overthrow the religion of the gods." Near Antipas stood a heathen altar. The prefect said to Antipas: "Will you renounce Christ, burn incense on the altar, and bow before the image of Caesar?" Antipas answered: "I cannot burn incense on the altar. I cannot bow to the image of Caesar. I bow only to God. I am a Christian." Immediately the amphitheater shook with the shout which soon was to be so familiar in all the arenas of the Roman world: *"Christianos ad leones!"*—"The Christians to the lions!" Antipas is led to the center of the arena, which all the attendants now vacate. A sliding door is raised from one of the subterranean cages at the lower end of the arena, and two famished lions rush forth. Soon it is all over. The hooting mob has dispersed to their homes. In the midst of the arena, just a few bones and a torn, bloodstained robe. But today, nineteen hundred years after Antipas gave his life for his faith, his name still lives, and we hear Christ say to that church at Pergamos, and to the whole Church throughout the world, throughout the ages: "Antipas, . . . my faithful martyr, who was slain among you, where Satan dwelleth."

Antipas is a sermon in a name, and a great sermon he is. He draws his own lesson, preaches his own sermon. Christ still calls for men like Antipas, and to them he still makes the same promise that he made to Antipas, and others like him, in that wicked city: "To him that overcometh will I give to eat of the hidden manna, and will give him a white stone, and in the stone a new name written, which no man knoweth saving he that receiveth it." That hidden manna is none other than Christ himself, the bread of life; and that white stone is the stone of acquittal in the day of judgment, and acceptance and honor with God.

XII

STEPHEN—THE MAN WHO LOOKED LIKE AN ANGEL

> "And all that sat in the council . . . saw his face as it had been the face of an angel."
>
> ACTS 6:15

EVERY MAN HAS WITHIN HIM THE POSSIBILITIES OF AN angel. These enraged enemies of Stephen, when they gnashed their teeth against him at the meeting of the Sanhedrin, and probably also when they were stoning him, saw his face as if it had been the face of an angel. That is a great tribute when you consider it came from men who wanted to kill him.

One of Rembrandt's famous paintings is that of himself, which is to be seen in the National Gallery in London. Every man produces one masterpiece—himself. Day and night, year in and year out, in conscious and unconscious moments, his words and deeds, his secret desires, what he permits or refuses, every hope, every fear, every purpose— all are strokes of the brush, and produce the painting. One day the canvas is finished. Death frames it and puts it on exhibition. Then not a line can be erased or changed, not a feature retouched or altered. The work is finished. There is the masterpiece, a masterpiece because it is absolutely true to life.

Here we have Stephen's unveiling. Here suddenly, dramatically, at the end of Stephen's life, his masterpiece is unveiled. And what a lovely portrait it is—like an angel.

Even his hating, bloodthirsty enemies had to confess that he looked like an angel. They had been looking for a traitor, a blasphemer; but what they saw instead was the face of an angel.

> He heeded not reviling tones,
> Nor sold his heart to idle moans,
> Tho' cursed and scorn'd, and bruised with stones;
>
> But looking upward, full of grace,
> He pray'd, and from a happy place
> God's glory smote him on the face.

One of the seven deacons appointed by the Church, Stephen had proved himself a mighty preacher of the gospel. In order to silence him his enemies haled him before the Sanhedrin on the charge that he spoke blasphemous words against the law and against Moses. In a memorable speech Stephen defended himself against this charge and denounced those who resisted the truth and who sought to slay him. After the trial he was dragged out and stoned, while Paul held the clothes of those who stoned him.

There are several remarkable things about this death and martyrdom of Stephen. One is that, with the exception of Christ himself, this is the only death in the Bible which is related with any degree of detail. The greatest followers of Christ are dismissed at the end of their life with hardly a word, as when, for example, the Book of Acts tells us that Herod killed James, the brother of John, with the sword. John himself, Peter and Paul, all pass from the stage of the New Testament without a word as to how they died; whereas the death of Stephen is related in full and unforgettable manner. Another remarkable thing about this death of Stephen is the beautiful prayer which he made for his murderers when he was dying, the prayer which not a few, among them Luther and Augustine, thought was used by the Holy Spirit for the conversion of Paul, who undoubtedly heard it.

But in some respects the most remarkable thing in this remarkable trial and martyrdom is what is recorded of Stephen when he was arraigned before the Sanhedrin, how that all they that sat in the council, looking steadfastly on him, "saw his face as it had been the face of an angel." This is said of Stephen at his trial, rather than when he was stoned. But I have no doubt that this description of Stephen belongs not exclusively to the account of the trial, but also to the account of his death. How dramatic is that record! His savage, cursing enemies, shouting for his blood, were silent and awe-struck for a moment as they marveled at the light in Stephen's face, for they seemed to see the face, not of a man, but of an angel, a more than mortal and earthly being, one who had the power and the light and glory of the other world in his face. Who knows but it was that look which Paul could never forget that was the means under God for Saul's conversion, just as much as the beautiful prayer of forgiveness for his murderers?

Man's highest destiny, Christ said, is to be as the angels in heaven. Here, then, we have set forth the angelic possibilities in human nature. They "saw his face as it had been the face of an angel." The face is often spoken of as the mirror of the soul; and how perfectly, quickly, inexorably, sadly, or beautifully the face pictures what is in the heart. If his murderers saw in the face of Stephen something that looked like an angel, that was only the reflection of what was in the heart of Stephen. What, then, was it in the character of Stephen which produced and brought forth that angelic look?

STEPHEN'S FAITH

Stephen was the first to die for his Christian faith. He was inspired, illuminated, and strengthened by faith. Faith lifted him far above the sea of raging, angry faces about him, and he saw Jesus at the right hand of God. His faith lifted him up, and he caught the reflection of the glory that is in the face of Jesus Christ.

It is faith that lifts man up to his highest and reveals him at his greatest. Man was created to see more than he can see with the naked eye, and to reach further than he can reach with his outstretched hand. Stephen was strong in this great battle at the end of his life because he was strong in his faith. Like Moses, he endured as seeing him who is invisible. And they always endure the longest and battle most triumphantly who are able to see the invisible.

Faith is the secret of all great accomplishments. It was Stephen's faith that made him eloquent, made him bold, made him Christlike. It was faith that brought the angelic look into Stephen's face. The angels, Christ told us, behold the face of God; and faith sees God in human life and in the affairs of the world. That is the great need of our life, that we should be able to see God, that we should know that he is here.

> Thrice blessed is he to whom is given
> The instinct that can tell
> That God is on the field
> When he is most invisible.

John said, "This is the victory that overcometh the world, even our faith." When Jesus warned Peter and told him that he would pray for him, what he prayed for was that his faith might not fail. We can undergo any loss in life but that. That is the supreme disaster—if your faith fails you.

STEPHEN'S COURAGE

Another thing that made Stephen look like an angel was his courage. There could be nothing grander than Stephen's solitary stand for Christ and the church. The apostles and all the other early Christian disciples disappear from our view at this time, and the Holy Spirit asks us to concentrate our thought and our gaze on Stephen. It is Stephen alone against the world, against all the enemies of Christ. He is put forward on this stage to stand and to speak for God, and how grandly he did it! What could be grander than his prophetlike denunciation of the enemies of God and of Christ, when he cried out in the tumult of the Sanhedrin, "Which of the prophets have not your fathers persecuted? And they have slain them which showed before of the coming of the Just One; of whom ye have been now the betrayers and murderers"? The face of Stephen lighted up like an angel because the angels speak for God. They are his ministers that do his will.

Stephen might have uttered some harmless platitudes when he stood before those raging fanatics and bigots at the Sanhedrin; or he might have said the difference between himself and them was, as some modern deniers of Christ say, only a difference in terms, in interpretation. But instead of that he declared unto them the truth of the living God, and denounced them as the resisters of the Holy Spirit and the betrayers and murderers of Jesus. He had the courage that Daniel had when he was brought in at midnight to the banqueting hall of Belshazzar and was asked to interpret the handwriting on the wall, which the drunken king and none of his lords and nobles or philosophers could read. Daniel might have said that he could not read it either. He might have given it an altogether false interpretation. Or he might have toned down its words of doom and judgment. But instead of that, this is what he said: "Mene; God hath numbered thy kingdom, and finished it." "Tekel; Thou art weighed in the balances, and art found wanting." "Peres; Thy kingdom is divided, and given to the Medes and Persians." Stephen had the courage that John the Baptist had when he went into the palace of Herod, and in the presence of Herodias said, "It is not lawful for thee to have her." Stephen had the courage that the prophet Nathan had when he went before David and told him the parable of the merciless and cruel rich man who had slain for his table and his guest the lamb of the poor man, and when David's anger was aroused against such a monster, said to him, "Thou art the man."

Standing in the midst of the throng at Stephen's trial and Stephen's death, we look once more upon the marvelous, heroic, angelic countenance; and as we look, lo, others rise suddenly up to stand by the side of Stephen. Look! There is Polycarp, the heroic bishop of Smyrna, standing by the fagots which will soon be lighted to consume him, and saying that he will never deny Christ, whom he has loved and served for more than eighty years. Look! There is John Huss at Constance, praying to Jesus as Stephen did, and asking him to receive his spirit. Looking upon Huss you think of those words on his magnificent monument at Prague, "Live for truth, fight for truth, die for truth." Look again! There is Martin Luther with the same heavenly light playing on his countenance, and we

[137]

hear him exclaim, "Here I stand; so help me God, I cannot otherwise!" It is by that light, the light of sublime courage and of loyalty to God, that the world marches onward and upward. Whenever men speak for truth and fight for truth, and, like Stephen, die for truth, there their voices have an angelic ring and their faces glow with the angelic light.

Sometimes when your Christian faith seems to be growing a little dim and your Christian character and witness seems anything but strong and robust, the best cure for it, the best tonic for it, the best way to restore it and strengthen it, will be to take, as you all have opportunity to take in the experiences of your daily life, an uncompromising and bold and courageous stand for Christ and the great principles of the Christian faith and of Christian life and conduct. That is a divine vitamin which never fails to revive and strengthen Christian faith.

STEPHEN'S LOVE

Stephen's faith and Stephen's courage were not in themselves sufficient to produce the angelic look on his face. Something else was necessary, and that was love. Paul said that a man might have all faith so that he could remove mountains, and might have all zeal and courage, but still be nothing because he has not love. The angels love. They love as God loves; hence the light on their faces. In that great scene in the *Tale of Two Cities,* when Sidney Carton went to the guillotine, taking the place of another for the love he bore for a woman, it was said about the city that night that "his was the peacefulest man's face ever beheld at the guillotine." Many added, that he looked sublime and prophetic. Love transfigures the countenance.

Stephen denounced his enemies and his murderers for

their hardness of heart, for their persecution of the prophets, and for their persecution and crucifixion of Christ, the Just One. But there is no hate or vengeance in his heart. So far as their personal injury to him is concerned, he would not have his sufferings and death held up against them. If possible, he would relieve them and save them from that judgment. And so he prayed, "Lord, lay not this sin to their charge." And when he had said this he fell asleep. When men reach that heavenly state of mind it is time for them to go. Thus it is, said Jesus, that we become sons of God. "Love your enemies, bless them that curse you, do good to them that hate you, and pray for them which despitefully use you and persecute you, that ye may be the children of your Father which is in heaven." Stephen's marvelous forgiving love lifted him up to the rank of the angels.

Joseph Parker, at one time the celebrated preacher in London City Temple, as a young man used to debate on the town green with infidels and atheists. One day an infidel shouted at him, "What did Christ do for Stephen when he was stoned?" Parker replied, with an answer which, he said, came to him like an inspiration from heaven, "He gave him grace to pray for those who stoned him." Stephen's prayer for those who stoned him was in reality a greater evidence of the power and presence of Christ in his life than any miracle of deliverance would have been.

How fares it then with the angels within you? Cultivate the angel within that his light may appear without. Every indulgence, every meanness, every dishonesty, every self-betrayal, every refusal of the good, every cowardly deed or word, every act of falsehood or passion or cruelty is a stroke of the brush which blots out the angel in your face. But every refusal of evil, every pure desire, every generous act, every sigh of pity, every word of truth and honor, is a stroke of the brush which brings out the angel look on the face.

Christ came to release and set free the angel which is in man. Stephen's faith in Christ, his companionship with him and his love for him, made him look like an angel because Christ had released the angelic powers in his soul. Many of you, no doubt, have portraits or photographs of your mother. One was taken when she was a girl, or a young bride; the other was taken in her old age. You cherish both portraits. The one taken in childhood or in young womanhood may be pleasing and beautiful; but the one that you cherish most is the one taken in old age, because the sorrows and self-denials, and prayers and faith of the years, have brought out the angelic look on your mother's face.

Stephen was a good and a devout man, we are told. Yet he looked like an angel. The same possibilities lie within us all. Remember it was not only this good, devout man that looked like an angel, but that thief and murderer on the cross. The angelic look was in his face too when he repented and asked Jesus to remember him when he came in his Kingdom. In the companionship of Christ men so totally different, a good, moral and devout man like Stephen, and a cruel murderer like that thief on the cross, can take on the angelic look. Let us think highly, therefore, of our great and possible destiny. Let us ask Christ to show his power in our souls, to drive out all that is evil and satanic, and let the angel go free. No sea of glass mingled with fire, no radiant sunrise, no flowers of the field arrayed with a splendor beyond that of Solomon in all his glory, no snow-covered mountaintop gilded with the setting sun, can compare for a moment with the beauty of the human face when it is lighted up by the spirit of Jesus Christ.

We have been speaking thus far of what the angry men of the Sanhedrin saw when they looked that day upon the face of Stephen, how it seemed to them that it was the face of an angel. But we must not forget something that Stephen himself saw that day. Standing there in the midst of his enemies who were raging against him, and gnashing their teeth on him and stoning him, he looked steadfastly up into heaven. He saw the glory of God, and Jesus standing on the right hand of God. That lets us know that Stephen had his exceeding great and high reward. He had the consciousness of the divine presence and the divine help. None of the men of the Sanhedrin could see what he saw, the glory of God. Paul could not see, as he was holding the garments of them that stoned him, what Stephen saw, the glory of God, and Jesus standing at the right hand of God. That is the vision that God grants to those who are faithful to him. "Be thou faithful unto death, and I will give thee a crown of life."

> "The soul that on Jesus hath leaned for repose
> I will not, I will not desert to his foes."

XIII

THOMAS—THE MAN WHO WAS NOT THERE

> "Blessed are they that have not seen, and yet have believed."
>
> JOHN 20:29

THAT IS THE LAST BEATITUDE OF OUR LORD. IN THE Sermon on the Mount he said: "Blessed are ye, when men shall . . . persecute you"; "Blessed are the peacemakers"; "Blessed are they which do hunger and thirst after righteousness"; and "Blessed are the pure in heart." Now you must add this last beatitude to the others. His ministry of humiliation and reconciliation over, ere he is received up into glory Christ says to his disciples: "Blessed are they that have not seen, and yet have believed."

The two disciples, Cleopas and his unnamed companion, with whom Jesus had talked on the road to Emmaus, and to whom he had revealed himself by the breaking of bread, had hurried back to Jerusalem and went at once to the chamber where they knew the apostles would be meeting. They were met with the word that Christ was risen and had appeared unto Peter. They replied with their own great tidings that he had made their hearts burn within them on the road to Emmaus, and that he had revealed himself unto them by the breaking of bread and then vanished out of their sight. While they are excitedly and with rejoicing telling the great tidings and wondering where next and to whom next their Lord will appear, sud-

[142]

denly Jesus stands in the midst of them, and, lifting his hands over them, says, "Peace be unto you." And "then were the disciples glad;" and that gladness has never yet faded out of the world, and never will fade away, until we shall behold him in glory.

THE ABSENT THOMAS

But there was one of the disciples, Thomas, who was not there. As if he was surprised at it, John takes particular pains to note that fact. "But Thomas, one of the twelve, called Didymus, was not with them when Jesus came." Together with Peter, Andrew, John, and Judas, Thomas is one of the five most sharply etched characters among the twelve apostles. This is due entirely to John's words about him, for his is the only one of the four Gospels which tells us anything of Thomas, other than that he was one of the twelve. The first light we have thrown on Thomas was when Jesus had gone into retirement in the country beyond the Jordan when the Jews were threatening his life. He announced that he would go to Jerusalem. Realizing the danger of this, Thomas said: "Let us also go, that we may die with him." He thought Jesus would be put to death if he went to Jerusalem, but he says, "Nevertheless, let us go with him and die with him."

The next word we have about Thomas was at the Lord's Supper. In his beautiful farewell address to the disciples Jesus said, "I go to prepare a place for you, . . . and whither I go ye know, and the way ye know." At this Thomas interrupted him and said bluntly, "We know not whither thou goest; and how can we know the way?" It was as if he had said: "What is the use of talking about the way when we do not know where you are going?" These somewhat melancholy and gloomy utterances of

[143]

Thomas in a way prepare us for the fact which is noted by John in his account of that first appearance of Jesus to the disciples, that Thomas was not there.

Let us see what Thomas missed. He missed the fellowship of his friends among the apostles. Even if there had been no appearance of Jesus that night, still his friends and disciples found comfort in talking with one another. There is no fellowship like the fellowship of Christ's followers. In any congregation there are people who come from different walks of life and different circumstances, and different training and background, but there is always one common bond, and that is they are one in their love for Christ. Let us always think of that bond when we come into the church. That is why the Apostle Peter tells us to "love the brotherhood."

Another thing that Thomas missed that night was the instruction that Jesus gave them, that great sermon that he preached on the meaning of his death and resurrection. Luke tells us about that. "Then opened he their understanding, that they might understand the scriptures, and said unto them, Thus it is written, and thus it behoved Christ to suffer, and to rise from the dead the third day: and that repentance and remission of sins should be preached in his name among all nations, beginning at Jerusalem. And ye are witnesses of these things."

Thomas missed also the commission that Christ gave the apostles. He outlined their work and their duty for them and said, "As my Father hath sent me, even so send I you." All that Thomas missed you can sum up by saying that he missed Christ, and the peace and the joy that Christ bestowed upon the disciples that night.

But not only did Thomas by his absence miss all this, but he put himself on the side of the enemies of Christ, the chief priests, the scribes, and the elders, who said that he was an imposter. Some of the neighbors noted the absence of Thomas. Perhaps one of them said: "I saw Peter going up to the room, and Matthew and John and Andrew, but I did not see Thomas. He does not take any more stock in it than I do." Satan and the enemies of Christianity do not ask you to scoff, to blaspheme, to proclaim that Christianity is false. All they ask you to do is what Thomas did, to stay away from the assembly of his disciples. But Thomas was not there. Suppose when Christ arose all had stayed away?

THE RETURN AND CONVICTION OF THOMAS

There is no doubt that Thomas has been overpraised as a fine type of the thoughtful and reverent doubter who must slowly find his way to a living faith. We are glad indeed that among the apostles there was one in particular who was unwilling to believe in the resurrection of Jesus. But so were all the others, we are told. But the particular reluctance of Thomas, together with the reluctance of the other disciples, disposes of the idea that the apostles were hallucinated visionaries, ready to believe anything they heard.

But the skepticism of Thomas bordered on defiance. The other apostles had refused to believe at first on the evidence of the women, but Thomas refuses to believe on the testimony of the ten apostles. He did not say: "If I see his wounds, the print of the nails in his hand, the mark of the lance in his side, I will believe," but, "I will not believe *unless* I see the print of the nails and put my hand in his side."

However, Thomas did not cut himself off completely from the twelve. We must give him credit for that, for the next Lord's day he was present. And the ten apostles were evidently kind and tolerant in their attitude toward Thomas. Because you are troubled with doubt about some doctrine or fact of the Christian faith is no reason why you should cut yourself off, or be cut off, from Christian fellowship or worship. Follow the light and the truth that you have, and more will come to you. If we know we shall follow on to know the Lord, and unto the upright there ariseth light in darkness. Let your prayer be that of the father whose boy Christ healed, "Lord, I believe; help thou mine unbelief."

The evening of the second Lord's day has come, and full of expectation the apostles gather in that same upper chamber where Jesus had appeared to them the week be-before. Here they come—Peter, no doubt full of energy and impulse, the first to arrive; and after him John, then Andrew, then James and Matthew and all the others, and last of all Thomas comes in. I am sure they were all glad when they saw Thomas. They had hardly exchanged their greetings when Jesus again stood in their midst and lifted his hands in peace over them.

Perhaps they wondered what Thomas would say, or what he would have to say to Jesus. They were not long left in doubt. Turning to Thomas, and with full knowledge of what he had said, and the defiance of his demand, Jesus said to Thomas: "Reach hither thy finger, and behold my hands; and reach hither thy hand, and thrust it into my side; and be not faithless, but believing." There is nothing to indicate that Thomas availed himself of Christ's invitation, or actually scrutinized the wounds of Jesus. The words and the presence of the Saviour were enough for him, and bowing before him Thomas exclaimed, "My Lord and my God!" It was reserved for the chief doubter

[146]

among the apostles to make the greatest personal profession that any of them made. Peter had confessed, "Thou art the Christ, the Son of the living God"; but here Thomas confesses, not only that Christ has arisen, not only that he is God and Lord, but "My Lord and my God." It is the once chief doubter who puts on the lips of all faithful disciples of Jesus the confession of their faith, *"My Lord and my God."* Can you say today what Thomas did?

THE LAST BEATITUDE

After Thomas had uttered his beautiful confession of faith, Jesus said to him: "Thomas, because thou hast seen me, thou hast believed: blessed are they that have not seen, and yet have believed." Our Lord did not mean that Thomas was not blessed, or that others were necessarily more blessed than he, for everyone who believes is blessed, and everyone who has seen the Lord, in the flesh or in faith, is blessed. What he meant was that all those who did not see him in the Resurrection, as Thomas did and as the other apostles did, and yet believe on him, are equally blessed. Christ looks forward to all those who hereafter shall believe on his name. Only a few men actually saw him in the Resurrection. The great multitude of Christians have never seen him save by the eye of faith. Looking forward to all those disciples out of every kingdom and age and race who confess his name until he shall come again, Christ pronounces upon them this great benediction.

Sometimes you may have a tendency to long for sight instead of faith. You may say to yourself: "If I had only seen some of those miracles. If I had seen him take the daughter of Jairus by the hand and raise her up. If I had seen him stop the funeral procession at Nain and restore the widow's son. If I had seen him open the eyes of Bartimaeus, or if I had seen him and heard him after his resurrection, as Peter and John and Thomas did, or if I could see him now, as I see you, then I would have no difficulty in believing on him, and even though I do believe on him now, my faith, by such confirmation, would be much stronger."

Are you sure of that? Christ makes it plain that we are at no disadvantage as compared with those who saw those miracles and heard Christ in the resurrection. Indeed it may be that if anyone has the advantage, it is we ourselves.

To his disciples and the men of his day Christ had to appear as a man who was sometimes weary, thirsty, hungry, just like themselves, a man who wore the same flowing robes that everyone else did and who spake the Aramaic dialect like all the others. You would like to see Christ now in the flesh? But just how would you see him? Of what race would he be? What language would he speak? What garments would he wear? A thousand difficulties arise the moment you think of Christ in the way the apostles and those who believed on him when he was on earth had to see him. But now, for you and me, all those difficulties of the visible, the material, the temporal, are done away, and with the believers of age after age witnessing and believing before us we confess, "Thou art my Lord and my God."

This kind of faith is sure and certain. One of the romances of the heavens is the story of the discovery of the planet Neptune, the outermost of known planets, as related by Professor Simon Newcomb. Up to that time the planet Uranus, discovered in 1781, had been regarded as the outermost of the planets. The study of Uranus by the astronomers revealed certain deviations and perturbations for which they could not account by any of the known laws and theories. Then they began to wonder if these perturbations might not arise from the action of another planet. They got to work with their mathematics and their theories, and finally reached the conclusion that the disturbances which they had noted in Uranus must be due to the action of an unknown planet. Then they located on their charts the place in the heavens where that planet must be. Finally, after midnight on the morning of September 14, 1846, an astronomer turned his instrument on the place designated and the great planet swam into view. The theories upon which they followed their investigations and finally discovered the planet were, of course, based upon observed data; nevertheless it was faith in the laws of the universe, and in the fidelity of those laws, which led them to discover the great planet. The eyes of the mind, the eye of faith, discovered it long before it was seen through the lens of the telescope.

What of the future life? What of the world of life beyond this world of sense, of touch, of shadow, and illusion? Sometimes you may be tempted to say: "If the curtain that veils that world were lifted only for a moment; if I could only see just for a moment my loved ones in that world and how they are, then I should feel much stronger in my faith about the life to come."

> Ah, Christ, that it were possible
>   For one brief hour
> To see the souls we love,
>   That they might tell us
>   What and where they are!

But are you sure your faith in immortality would be stronger then? Once a woman whose worthy husband had died, and who was a woman of real Christian faith, told me that in some sort of a vision, as it were, she had clearly seen her husband. There was no particular comfort in what he said, or in the state in which she saw him, but she felt that it brought a certain assurance of the fact of life after death.

But here again Christ says, "Blessed are they that have not seen, and yet have believed." I would not say that it is impossible that God should permit some to see into that world before they enter it. But if they did, I cannot see how they are more blessed than the great majority of us who must rest in faith. I do not know that I would believe more earnestly in the existence of friends who have passed into the unseen world if I had some vision of them in that now hidden and unknown state, than I do now, not having seen, but resting in the words and in the life of the risen Christ himself, the first fruits of them that slept. Paul saw into heaven, was taken up into the third heaven, and yet it is Paul himself who says that here we must walk by faith. "Blessed are they that have not seen and yet have believed."

Blessed are they who, although they cannot see the far-off victory of Christ, believe in it. The world's horizon is dark today. Nations have been subjugated and robbed of that which makes life most worth living. Evil everywhere seems in the ascendency. We think of our own nation as one of the few remaining custodians and defenders of democracy and liberty, as indeed, thank God, it is. But how much crime and wickedness and godlessness there is in the United States everywhere today. Can you and I believe in the triumph of justice and righteousness? Can we see the victory of truth? Here again Christ pronounces his benediction upon those who have not seen, yet have believed, who have indeed seen the glory of the coming of the Lord, but have seen it only with the eye of faith.

I stood once on little Patmos, that brown gem in the Aegean Sea. But all that I saw was the brown mountain, the turquoise sea; and all that I heard was the gentle washing of the waves and the soft chiming of the bells of St. John's Monastery. I did not see what John saw there, the star Wormwood falling from heaven, the four horsemen going forth, the woman clothed in the sun, Satan bound for a thousand years, and then finally cast into the abyss. I did not see the white horse and his rider going forth to conquer as John saw it; nor did I hear the blast of the trumpets of revelation and judgment. I did not see the new heaven and the new earth; and the New Jerusalem coming down from God out of heaven, like a bride adorned for her husband. Yet Christ said, in effect: "Blessed are they who have not seen, yet have believed, have such faith in me that they never doubt the victory of righteousness and truth, and never doubt the glorious consummation, compared with which the brightest day that has dawned upon the world is midnight and the fairest splendors which have invested it but the shadow of darkness."

Peter himself, who heard Jesus say that to Thomas, "Blessed are they that have not seen, and yet have believed," said practically the same thing to the believers of his day. He exhorted the persecuted Christians to be faithful to the end, that they be found unto praise and honor and glory at the appearing of Christ, "Whom," he says, "having not seen, ye love; in whom, though now ye see him not, yet believing, ye rejoice with joy unspeakable and full of glory: receiving the end of your faith, even the salvation of your souls."

Peter was one of those who saw and believed, but he claims no advantage over those who have not seen and yet have believed. They too can rejoice with joy unspeakable and full of glory. Let us rejoice, then, in the Saviour whom we have not seen and yet love. Let us believe that he is our Redeemer from sin and from death. Let us believe that his Kingdom shall come and his will be done. Christ knew the finalities, he knew the realities, and he said it, for you and for me, "Blessed are they that have not seen, and yet have believed." There is no true blessedness in life without faith in God and in his Son Jesus Christ. Are you one of those of whom Christ can say: "Blessed are they that have not seen, and yet have believed"?

XIV

ANDREW—THE MAN WHO BROUGHT HIS BROTHER

> "He first findeth his own brother Simon, . . . and he brought him to Jesus."
>
> JOHN 1:41-42

THE BASILICA OF ST. PETER AT ROME IS, FOR MANY reasons, the world's most notable place of worship. It is notable first of all for its site, for it stands on the very place where the Emperor Nero drove his chariot by night through his gardens, his way illuminated by the blazing pitch-covered bodies of the Christian martyrs. It is notable for its chief architect and builder, Michelangelo; for the triumphs of sculpture and painting which adorn it; for its gloomy crypt, where sleep the long succession of the bishops of Rome, and, according to the ancient tradition, Peter himself. It is notable for the vastness of its area and the years of its construction; for the famous statue of Peter, worn smooth by the kisses of devout pilgrims from every quarter of the globe; for the prayers for grace and forgiveness that are daily offered there by sinners in every language spoken by man since the confusion of tongues at the Tower of Babel. It is notable for its great golden dome, surmounted by the cross, and which, seen afar off by the traveler coming from the north or the south, the east or the west, lets him know that he is approaching the Eternal City. Within and around that great dome are the words of Christ to Peter: "Thou art Peter, and upon

[153]

this rock I will build my church; and the gates of hell shall not prevail against it." But standing under that great dome, and reading those words from Matthew's Gospel, there is another inscription that one feels ought to be added. It is this sentence from John's Gospel: "He first findeth his own brother Simon, . . . and he brought him to Jesus." Without Andrew there would have been no Peter.

That is the greatest present need of the Church—more Andrews, more men who will tell the news of Christ and bring others to him. Since the great work of the ministry, and indeed of every Christian, is to witness for Christ, and to bring others to him, one of the most profitable things we can do is to study for a little the history of this man Andrew.

> Who art thou that wouldst grave thy name
> Thus deeply in a brother's heart?
> Look on this saint, and learn to frame
> Thy love charm with true Christian art.[1]

ANDREW BROUGHT HIMSELF TO CHRIST

The story of that first meeting of Andrew and Christ is related by John in his Gospel. It was the second day after the baptism of Jesus by John the Baptist. Andrew and another disciple of the Baptist, whom John does not name, but whom it is easy to identify as John himself, were talking with John the Baptist when Jesus passed by. As he passed the Baptist said to these two men: "Behold the Lamb of God!" Struck with that great description, Andrew and John turned to follow Jesus. I feel sure that it was Andrew who made the suggestion, when he heard

[1] John Keble, *The Christian Year.*

the Baptist speak, that they follow Jesus and learn more of him; and if so, then Andrew has the great distinction of having brought not only Peter but also John to Jesus.

Andrew wrote no Gospel. But if he had, I have no doubt his recollection of that day would have been as clear as that of John, who, writing perhaps half a century later, still remembered all the incidents of that memorable day, just where they were standing, in whose company they were, and how high the sun was in the heavens, for he says that "it was about the tenth hour." There were other great hours in John's life: the hour of Christ's transfiguration on the mountaintop, the hour in Gethsemane, the hour of the crucifixion, the hour of his appearance to the disciples by the Sea of Galilee after his resurrection, the hour of his ascension into the heavens, and the hour when John saw him standing amid the seven golden candlesticks in glory on the Isle of Patmos. But this is the one hour which John remembered above all others—that hour when he and Andrew followed Jesus and talked with him.

It was about the tenth hour! Above the usual run of hours there are what we might describe as "tenth hours" of opportunity and decision; hours when what we decide or fail to decide, what we permit or refuse, what we say or do not say, what we do or do not do, has a never-ebbing influence upon the soul. The destiny which proceeds and flows from these "tenth hours" is determined partly by the divine Providence which brings a man face to face with that hour, and partly by the action, the decision of the man who passes through that hour. John and Andrew had their "tenth hour" when there on the banks of the Jordan they heard John the Baptist say of Jesus as he passed by: "Behold the Lamb of God!" and both of them immediately made use of that hour. Thus for their souls that hour was forever memorable. The greatest hour for any soul is that hour when he finds Christ as his Saviour.

When Jesus knew that Andrew and John were following him he turned and said: "What seek ye?" And they, perhaps at a loss for something to say, answered: "Where dwellest thou?" Jesus said: "Come and see." So they went with him and saw and heard for themselves. What was said that day, the questions they asked and the answers Jesus gave, we do not know. But Andrew came away convinced that Jesus was the Christ.

On the great event of that day, in that turning point in the life of Andrew and John, the Baptist himself played an important part. What if John the Baptist, when he saw Jesus pass by that day, had said something else and something less about Jesus than he did say? What was it that the Baptist said of Christ? Did he say: "Behold the man who did no sin, and whose blameless life will leave the world a great example of how to live"? Did he say: "Behold the man, the carpenter's son who never wrote a line save in the dust, and yet the man whose words have done more to temper and soften and regenerate mankind than all the sayings of the philosophers and all the books of the sages"? Did he say: "Behold the man whose birth will be the watershed of history, dividing it into two parts, 'Before Christ' and 'After Christ' "? Did he say: "Behold the man whose life shall be a fountain of compassion whence shall flow the healing streams of mercy and pity"? Did he say: "Behold the man who was in the world, and yet not of it, and who more than any other has brought life and immortality to light"? Did he say: "Behold the man whose death on the cross will be the supreme example of that vicarious suffering which runs like a scarlet thread through all creation"? Was that what John said of Jesus?

[156]

If so, oblivion's sea had long ago swept over him. No, not that but this, this which takes all that in, this which left out, Christianity is left out: "Behold the Lamb of God, which taketh away the sin of the world."

ANDREW BROUGHT HIS BROTHER TO JESUS

Andrew had made a great discovery. Let us see what he did with it. He had great news to tell, and he hastened to tell it. Andrew "first findeth his own brother Simon, . . . and he brought him to Jesus." I wonder where it was he found Peter? Perhaps down by the riverside, or under one of the fig trees, or, if it was several days later, mending his nets by the seashore, or perhaps out in the boat on the Sea of Galilee. And Andrew went down to the water's edge, and, putting his hand to his mouth, shouted across the sea to Peter: "We have found the Messiah, the Christ of Israel!"

There was no doubt, no question mark, in Andrew's decisive, eager utterance. No halfway conviction would have brought Peter to Christ. Suppose Andrew had said: "I saw a man yesterday who I think may be the Christ. John the Baptist called him the Lamb of God. I am sure that at least he is a pure and noble character." That would never have brought Peter to Christ. Instead of that Andrew said: "We have found . . . the Christ!"

It was his own brother to whom Andrew first told the great news. It will often take more courage and faith and love to speak to a brother of Christ than to a man in China or India or Africa. Frequently I receive letters from parents or husbands or wives or brothers or sisters, asking me to take an interest in the spiritual welfare of someone dear to them. But often at the end of the request comes this word: "But do not let him know that I have asked you."

Why should that be? Those requests show faith, conviction, Christian love and concern, but also a strange unwillingness to do as Andrew did when first he brought his own brother. Sometimes the reason is a strange, indefinable shrinking from speaking on the greatest things to those nearest to us; but sometimes it is a sense of personal unworthiness, a consciousness of something in our life that would dull or cancel the power of our appeal.

It is clear that in Andrew's relationship with Peter there was nothing that made it awkward or embarrassing for him to speak to Peter about his soul and the soul's Saviour. On those long nights with the nets on the Sea of Galilee, or on the long journey up to Jerusalem to market the fish, there was nothing that Andrew had said or done which now rose up to silence him or to mock at him when he desired to speak to Peter about Christ. Our lives testify and influence others as well as our words. Mere good example in daily life, that alone cannot bring anyone to Christ, for the great story of redeeming love must be told, and its great invitation given. "Faith cometh," as Paul said, "by hearing." But the life and character of the man who speaks for Christ will back up and enforce, or weaken and cancel, his testimony when he seeks to bring another life to Christ. On one occasion an ambitious young monk desired to have Francis of Assisi teach him how to preach. Francis took him with him, and they left the monastery and walked for hours through the towns and in the country and then back to the monastery. The impatient monk said to Francis: "But you have not yet taught me how to preach!" Then Francis explained to him that there was the sermon of the life as well as of the mind and the heart and the tongue.

How careful, then, we ought to be, and what manner

[158]

of persons we ought to be, so that when we speak for Christ our life as well as our heart and mind and tongue will speak. How glad we ought to be to relinquish and forsake even things harmless in themselves, and perhaps harmless to us, but which might possibly cause someone else to stumble, or hurt our influence as a Christian. That was the high ground which Christ himself took when he said: "For their sakes [for the sake of my influence upon others], I sanctify myself."

ANDREW BROUGHT A BOY TO CHRIST

Andrew appears in action just four times in the Gospels, and every time he is bringing someone to Christ. This time it was a boy. A great multitude had followed Jesus around the head of the Sea of Galilee, where he taught them in a mountain. The multitude were far from home, and were tired and hungry. Jesus called Philip to him and said: "Whence shall we buy bread, that these may eat?" Astonished at such a question, Philip exclaimed: "Two hundred pennyworth of bread is not sufficient for them, that every one of them may take a little." But Andrew, who seems to have been often in Philip's company, overhearing what Jesus said, and what Philip answered, said to Jesus: "There is a lad here, who has five barley loaves, and two small fishes." Then he added: "But what are they among so many?" That was quite different, however, from the skepticism of Philip. All that Andrew meant was that it would be a wonderful thing indeed if Jesus could feed such a multitude with five loaves and two small fishes. But evidently there was in his mind the thought: "Who knows? He can do it if he will." Jesus then told Andrew to bring up the boy; and that boy's five loaves and two small fishes, multiplied by the power of Christ, fed the multitude.

That boy, to whom no one but Andrew paid any attention that day, was the most important one of the five thousand in that crowd, and more important too than the twelve disciples. A boy is always of great importance. Wherever you can say "There is a boy here," whether at the church service, or on the football field, or in the home, or in the Sunday-school class, there is the possibility of great things for the Kingdom of God. When you talk of trying to influence others for Christ, do not forget the boy. One boy may mean a host.

In a Congregational manse in England a returned missionary to Russia was the guest in the minister's home. Visiting there at the time was a lad who was the grandson of the minister. One night after evening worship the missionary, who had been taken with the lad, asked him to point out the chamber where he slept. Early in the morning he called him, and as they sat together in the garden he told him of the love of Christ. A few days later, when he was about to leave the home, and as they were concluding family worship, the missionary took the boy on his knee and said to those assembled: "I am convinced that this boy will preach the gospel. I am convinced that he will be a great preacher of the gospel, and that he will stand one day in the pulpit of Rowland Hill." Then he said to the boy, as he gave him a shilling: "I want you to promise that when that day comes, and you stand in Rowland Hill's pulpit, you will give out the hymn 'God Moves in a Mysterious Way His Wonders to Perform.'"

Several years have passed by, and the minister's grandson, now a lad of sixteen, is on his way to church in Colchester. A storm came up and he turned into the Primitive

Methodist Chapel in Artillery Street. The regular minister did not appear, and a layman, whose name is to this day unknown, arose in the pulpit and gave out the text from Isaiah 45:22: "Look unto me, and be ye saved, all the ends of the earth: for I am God, and there is none else." That boy sitting in the rear of the darkened and almost empty church answered the text and was saved. As he said six years afterward: "I looked that moment. The grace of faith was vouchsafed to me in the selfsame instant; and now I think I can say with truth:

> Ere since by faith I saw the stream
> Thy flowing wounds supply,
> Redeeming love has been my theme,
> And shall be till I die."

That boy was Charles H. Spurgeon!

One day an old minister in England walked into his churchyard, and sitting down on a tombstone began to weep. He wept because his church officers had just notified him that he was getting old and that he ought to resign and let a younger man take his place. As he sat there disconsolate he saw a boy with the sunshine in his face and joy in his heart coming down the street beyond the cemetery fence. The old preacher was fond of boys, and he called this boy to him and had him sit down beside him on the tombstone. There he forgot his own sorrow as he talked with the boy about the meaning of life and told him about Christ and his salvation. Presently the boy left him and went on his happy way down the street. The old preacher went back to his manse and to his sorrow. Not long afterward he was called to his eternal home, and if it is permitted the redeemed in the life to come to behold what transpires on earth, then this is what that old preacher would have seen. He would have seen that boy with whom he talked now a lay preacher, a teacher, and a cobbler. In his schoolroom and cobbler shop he has fashioned a large leather globe, and the scholars in his class and the customers who come in for their shoes will sometimes see the face of the teacher-cobbler suffused with emotion as he points to land after land on that globe and says, "And these are pagans!" A few more years have passed, and that boy to whom the old preacher talked that day in the cemetery is the pioneer missionary to India, and translating the Scriptures into the dialects of the East —William G. Carey.

Some time ago, visiting a nephew at Harvard University, I was taken to dine at a restaurant not far from Boston Common. As I was going through the doors into the restaurant I saw a tablet on the wall which said that on that spot, April 21, 1865, a certain famous preacher and evangelist was "converted to God." As I read the inscription my mind reverted to the day when Edward Kimball, a teacher in the Sunday school of the Mount Vernon Congregational Church, walked up and down in front of that shoe store where the restaurant now stands. The throngs of people were hurrying past him in the direction of the State House and Boston Common, but he turned and passed and repassed the shoe store. At length he mustered up his courage, and, walking rapidly into the store, asked for one of the boys in his class who was employed there. He found him in the back of the store, wrapping up a package of shoes, and, putting his hand on his shoulder, said to him: "Dwight, don't you think it is about time you gave your heart to the Lord?" It was time! It was the "tenth hour"; and that boy—Dwight L. Moody—gave his heart then and there to the Lord. Forty years afterward, preaching in Tremont Temple, a stone's throw from where that store stood, Moody said: "I remember the morning on which I came out of my room after I had first trusted Christ. I thought the old sun shone a good deal brighter than it ever had before—I thought that it was just smiling upon me; and as I walked out upon Boston Common, and heard the birds singing in the trees, I thought they were all singing a song for me. Do you know I fell in love with the birds. I had never cared for them before. It seemed to me that I was in love with all creation. I had not a bitter feeling against any man, and I was ready to take all mankind to my heart."

The half-educated lay preacher in the Primitive Methodist Chapel at Colchester brought a boy to Christ, and soon that boy, Charles H. Spurgeon, was feeding the thousands. The disconsolate old preacher, sitting on the tombstone in the English churchyard, told a boy of the love of Christ, and soon that boy was feeding the multitudes in India. The teacher in the Mount Vernon Street Congregational Sunday school asked a boy if it was not time for him to give his heart to Christ, and soon that boy, Dwight L. Moody, was feeding the multitudes.

ANDREW BROUGHT THE STRANGERS TO CHRIST

He brought Peter and he brought the boy; now he brings strangers to Christ. It was near the end of Christ's earthly life, some days after the resurrection of Lazarus, after the triumphal entry into Jerusalem, and just a few days before the Crucifixion. Among those who came up to the feast at Jerusalem were "certain Greeks." These Greeks came to Philip, perhaps because Philip had a Greek name and had Greek connections. They said to Philip those now memorable words: "We would see Jesus." In other words, would he introduce them to Christ? But Philip was not sure about that. Jesus was the Messiah of Israel. True, he had said great things about his universal ministry, and how he had other sheep not of this fold; but Philip had not understood those things any more than the other disciples had. Yet he was reluctant to turn these men away. He would ask one of the other disciples about it. And who was it that he asked? He did not go to Peter nor to John, for impetuous Peter and John, the sons of thunder, might have said: "Tell the Greeks to be gone! Christ has come to bring salvation to the house of Israel." No, he went to Andrew! And when Andrew heard what Philip had to say, that the Greeks wanted to see Jesus, without a moment's hesitation he took them to Jesus.

When Jesus saw them his soul was stirred with joy. He saw men coming into his Kingdom through all future generations, from the east and the west, from the north and the south. He saw Peter bringing them in on the Day of Pentecost. He saw Paul bringing them in at Antioch and Ephesus and Corinth and Athens. He saw Augustine bringing them in from England and Germany. He saw Moffatt and Livingstone bringing them in from Africa, and Morrison from China, and Gilmore from Mongolia, and John G. Paton from the South Seas. He saw them coming in, coming in, until the last elect soul has come home, and cried out in his joy and triumph: "I, if I be lifted up from the earth, will draw all men unto me. . . . Father, glorify thy Name."

Such a man, then, was Andrew, who, best of all among the apostles, tells us how to bring others to Christ, for he is the man who brought Peter, and all that Peter has meant to Christianity. What the Church needs is more Andrews.

Andrew wrote no Gospel, like John; no epistles, like Peter; worked, so far as we know, no great miracles; never preached a sermon like Peter preached on the Day of Pentecost, bringing three thousand souls to Christ; but he brought the man who worked the miracles and wrote the epistles and preached the great sermon. Peter and John and Paul cannot be reproduced. God made but one Peter, one Paul, and one John, and broke the die in making them. But Andrew can be reproduced; and if the Church is to go on and thrive and prosper, Andrew *must* be reproduced.

In Bulwer-Lytton's *Last Days of Pompeii,* there is a beautiful example of how the gospel spread and how one man told it to another. Glaucus, falsely charged with the crime of murder, was condemned to fight with a lion in the arena. He was led to the revolving door under the temple of Jupiter, and through the narrow opening was thrust into the dungeon. A pitcher of water and a loaf of bread were placed before him, the door was closed, and he was left in darkness. As the handsome young Athenian, suddenly thrust down to the lowest abyss of ignominy and horror, realized his plight, the bitterness of his soul gave vent in a groan of anguish. With that, a voice from the recess of the dungeon answered his groan: "Who is my companion in this awful hour? Athenian Glaucus, is it thou?" The speaker was Olynthus, only yesterday converted to Christianity, and now condemned as an atheist to fight with a tiger. Companions in danger, and both near to death, the Christian ex-gladiator and prizefighter crept near in the darkness to the side of the cultivated Greek, and hastened to tell him of his Christian faith; how his God was with him in the dungeon, how his smile penetrated the darkness, and how on the eve of death his heart whispered of immortality, and earth receded from him but to bring his weary soul nearer to heaven. "And there, as oft in the early ages, of the Christian creed, it was in the darkness of the dungeon, and over the approach of death that the dawning gospel shed its soft and consecrating rays."

That was the way it spread. The slave told it to his fellow slave, the soldier to his comrade, the merchant to the merchant, the sailor on the sea to another sailor, the slave to his master, and the maid to her mistress. Each told the other the glad tidings of redemption and of eternal hope in Christ, for each was convinced that he had something to tell. Andrew brought Peter, and Philip brought Nathanael, and down through the ages that is the way men have been coming to Christ.

In my vision I saw the King seated upon his throne, and on either side of the throne stood the great angels, Uriel, the Angel of Light, Raphael, the Angel of Reason, Michael, the Angel of the Sword, and Gabriel, the Angel of Holy Song. Before the throne stood another angel, the Angel of the Book, and by his side stood one of the mortals. The King on the throne said to the Angel of the Book: "Who is this that you have brought, and what are his claims?"

The angel looked in the book and said: "O King, this man was a great inventor, and shed light on the pathway of man through the world."

"Then," said the King on his throne, "send him up, and let him stand here by the side of Uriel, the Angel of Light." So he went up and stood by the side of Uriel.

Then the Angel of the Book brought another before the throne. The King looked on him and said: "Who is this, and what are his claims?"

The angel looked in the book and said: "This man was

a great philosopher, a thinker, who thought thy thoughts after thee."

Whereupon the King said: "Send him up, and let him stand here by the side of Raphael, the Angel of Reason." So he went up and stood by the side of Raphael.

Then the angel brought a third mortal before the throne. Looking upon him the King said: "Who is this, and what are his claims?"

The angel looked in the book and said: "This was a great patriot. With his sword he delivered his people out of the hand of the despots and tyrants."

Then the King said: "Send him up, and let him stand here by the side of Michael, the Angel of the Sword." So he went up and stood by the side of Michael.

Then the Angel of the Book brought before the throne a fourth mortal. The King looked upon him and said: "Who is this, and what are his claims?"

The angel looked in the book and answered: "This man sang holy songs in praise of God, songs which still echo through the Church of the living God."

The King said: "Send him up, and let him stand and sing here by the side of Gabriel, the Angel of Holy Song." So the man went up and stood and sang by the side of Gabriel, the singer of holy and prophetic song.

Then the angel brought before the throne a fifth mortal, and when I saw him I wondered who he was and why he had been brought before the throne, for in his person I saw no note of greatness and in his eye no flash of genius. Yet, when I looked a second time, in his countenance there was a light that distinguished him from all the rest. Looking upon him, the King said: "Who is this, and what are his claims?"

Then the angel looked in the book, and lifting his head to the King, said, "This man won a soul for Christ."

And that time I never heard what the King on his throne said, for all heaven rang with a great shout—angels and archangels, cherubim and seraphim, and all the host of the redeemed, rejoicing together over one soul that had been redeemed!

That highest of all distinctions is within the reach of every Christian man. "He that winneth souls is wise." "And they that be wise shall shine as the brightness of the firmament; and they that turn many to righteousness as the stars forever and ever."

XV

NAAMAN—THE MAN WHO WASHED AND WAS CLEAN

> "Then went he down, and dipped himself seven times in Jordan."
>
> II Kings 5:14

NAAMAN, THE CAPTAIN OF THE SYRIAN HOST, WAS DRESSing one morning to present himself at court. Stretching out his muscular, well-braceleted arm, his eye fell on something there which he had never seen before. He looked at it carefully, and as he did so the bronzed face of the veteran of many campaigns began to pale. But Naaman was a soldier, and, throwing his robes about him, he went to the court and performed his duties with the King Benhadad.

Some weeks later when he looked again the spot had grown larger. Another week or two passed by, and there was a spot on the other arm, and then one on his thigh. There was no doubt about it. Naaman was a leper! He had fallen a victim of mankind's oldest, most dreaded, most exclusively human, and most loathsome disease.

UNSUSPECTED SORROWS AND BURDENS

Naaman was a great man, but he was a leper. He was wealthy. He lived in a beautiful villa in the midst of a grove of fruit trees and sweet-scented bushes on the banks of the swiftly flowing Abana. He was famous as the leader of the armies of Syria and as the deliverer of his nation.

[169]

The king honored him and whenever he appeared in public the people hailed and saluted him. And yet he was a leper! Although he occupied the second place in the kingdom, he would have been glad to have exchanged places with any healthy soldier in his army.

There is always a "but" to human greatness and fame and pleasure. Many who may be the object of envy would be glad to part with all they have for a body free of disease, or a mind free of the reproach of conscience, or a life unshadowed by remorse or loneliness. Whatever the lot of man may be, there is always the other side, and the hidden side. In this respect Naaman is typical of human experience. Under the gorgeous robes of the satrap of Syria there were the hideous marks of the leper. So under bright and fair exteriors there often lies the hidden thorn in the flesh or in the spirit, some scar or secret misery. When David Livingstone was at the height of his fame as an explorer, and England welcomed him home as a hero, and scientific societies and universities were bestowing upon him medals and degrees, he had a wayward son Robert, who had drifted to the United States, enlisted in the Union army, and finally perished on the field of Gettysburg. In a letter to a friend written at that time Livingstone said: "My own son is in the Federal army in America, and no credit to me. How often when we appear to be sailing gloriously with the wind the invisible hand applies the secret ballast." How much of that secret ballast there is in life!

In one of the wars between Syria and Israel the capital of Israel was besieged and straitly shut up. The famine was severe in the city, and so bitter was the hunger that the head of an unclean and forbidden beast, the ass, was sold for eighty pieces of silver. In order to encourage the people to endure hardship and resist the foe, Jehoram walked along the walls of the city. As he made his rounds he was accosted by a woman who cried to him: "Help, my lord, O king!" The story she told him was this: She had made a bargain with a neighboring woman that on succeeding days they would kill and eat their sons. She had kept her part of the bargain and had killed her child and eaten him with the other mother. But now that the pangs of hunger were appeased, maternal feeling had reasserted itself in the second mother and she had hid her son. Amazed and horrified at what the woman told him, the king rent his clothes, and as he did so, those who were gathered about listening were surprised to see that he had sackcloth within. Underneath the purple and fine linen and the gorgeous uniform they saw upon the king's body the coarse rags of sackcloth.

That is a true parable of life. Under the bright exterior and the robes of prosperity and plenty we can see, when the wind of adversity lifts them, the somber colors of sackcloth. It was so with Naaman. On the outside a great man; but under his robes of office the flesh of a leper. It is well for us to remember this, for to do so will restrain our envy of others, for it will remind us that always in the one whom we envy there is something that none of us would desire for ourselves. It also teaches us kindness and sympathy, telling us that there may be trouble and sorrow and heartache where we little imagine it.

> If every man's internal care
>   Were written on his brow,
> How many who our envy share
>   Would have our pity now.

[171]

HOW GREAT SERVICE CAN BE RENDERED BY HUMBLE AGENTS

Naaman was fortunate in that there was in his home a slave girl who knew something of the true God and of his prophet Elisha. On one of the Syrian raids into the kingdom of Israel this little maid had been captured by the victorious army and carried off to Damascus, where she was sold to Naaman, who gave her for a house slave to his wife. This girl had been separated from her native land, carried away from her father and mother, her brothers and sisters and her friends and companions. No lot could seem to be worse. Yet it is plain that she was not embittered by her experience and that she had no harsh or revengeful feeling toward those who had taken her captive. She had learned of the sickness of her master Naaman, and one day she had said to her mistress when she was waiting upon her: "Would God my lord were with the prophet that is in Samaria! for he would recover him of his leprosy." This saying of the slave girl was reported to Naaman. He knew that he was a leper. He knew too that he had consulted all the physicians and tried all the cures, and was nothing bettered but rather worse. No doubt too he had heard something of Elisha, the famous prophet of Israel, and the wonders which he had wrought. Perhaps Naaman thought to himself: "He can cure me of my leprosy." With this in mind he went to the king and told him of what the damsel had said. When Benhadad heard of it he told Naaman he would write to Jehoram, the king of Israel, asking him to cure him of his leprosy.

Thus it was by the earnest word of a captive slave girl that Naaman was put in touch with the prophet of Israel and eventually cured of his leprosy. The providence of God worked through the kindness and sympathy and faith

[172]

of a slave girl. And thus Naaman was not only healed of his plague, but was converted from idolatry and became a worshiper of the true God. Small forces working at important beginnings produce great results. This was not the first time in Israel's history that such a thing had happened. When the princess royal of Egypt had taken out of the Nile the child Moses, whom she found floating there in his ark in the bulrushes, and wondered where she could find a nurse to bring up the child, the quick-witted maid, the sister of Moses, Miriam, came out from her hiding place and told the princess she knew of a good nurse. The nurse was none other than the mother of Moses herself. Where there is sympathy and love for our fellow man, where there is faith in God and faith in the power of Christ to comfort and strengthen and heal, there the humblest Christian may be able to do a great work for God.

THE FOLLY AND DANGER OF UNTIMELY ANGER

Armed with the letter of the king of Syria to the king of Israel, and taking with him fifty thousand dollars in gold and silver, and changes of costly raiment, Naaman and his cavalcade started on the journey southward for Samaria. When they reached the city, having come up the long, winding road by which one still ascends to the ruins of Samaria on the top of its mountain, Naaman presented himself and his letter to the king of Israel. When the King Jehoram had read the letter, which in a way was a command that he should see to it that Naaman was healed of his leprosy, Jehoram thought that Benhadad, the king of Syria, was seeking a quarrel with him, and another occasion for war, by asking him to do what only God could do, cleanse a leper. The king rent his garments, saying as he did so: "Am I God, to kill and to make alive?" But before Naaman left the city, Elisha learned of his presence and the errand on which he had come, and sent a message to the king, saying, "Wherefore hast thou rent thy clothes? let him come now to me, and he shall know that there is a prophet in Israel."

Naaman then drove through Samaria to the home of the prophet and drew up in front of his house. His chariot, decorated with silver and gold, and the beautiful Arabian horses champing their bits, the bright uniforms of Naaman's staff and his own gorgeous apparel—all was in strange contrast with the humble abode of the prophet. Naaman sent one of his servants in to tell Elisha what was wanted and who he was. After a little there came out of the house of the prophet, not Elisha himself, but his servant Gehazi! That gave Naaman a great shock. The second man in the Syrian empire was accustomed to send servants and messengers to other men, but he was not accustomed to have other men, even the greatest and most renowned, send a servant to him. They came in person. That was what Naaman expected of Elisha. But instead of that, Elisha sent his servant!

If the failure of Elisha to come in person offended the dignity and pride of Naaman, much more so did the message which the servant brought from Elisha. This was the message: "Go and wash in Jordan seven times, and thy flesh shall come again to thee, and thou shalt be clean." When he heard that, the anger of Naaman knew no bounds. Impetuously he cried out, in effect: "Behold, I thought he would come out to me, call upon the name of his God, and pass his hand over the place and heal me! But instead of that he sends a servant, and tells me to go down and wash in that wretched stream which I crossed yesterday on the way to this city, the River Jordan! If it is washing in a river that is going to heal me, I can do that at home. Are not Abana and Pharpar better than all the rivers of Israel?"

Having thus expressed himself, Naaman, in a great rage, cut his horses over their haunches with his whip, turned their heads about, and with the wheels of the chariot bounding up and down on the stones of the street, drove down the steep winding road into the valley below and off in the direction of Damascus, leaving behind him a murmur of Syrian profanity and a cloud of dust.

Again it was fortunate for Naaman that he had some wise soldiers and servants with him who were not afraid to speak to their lord in his own behalf. One of these now spoke to Naaman. By this time the rage of Naaman had spent itself somewhat. The horses had got over their excitement and were slowed down to a walk. Naaman handed the reins to one of his officers and sat wearily on his stool in the chariot. He remembered that after all he was still a leper. It was then that one of his servants spoke to him and said: "My father, if the prophet had bid thee do some great thing, wouldst thou not have done it? How much rather then, when he saith to thee, Wash, and be clean?" A word in season, how good it is! Naaman saw the sense of that at once. If Elisha had told him to go and wash in the Euphrates or the Tigris, or to climb Mount Hermon on his hands and knees, or to spend some vast sum of money, he would have done it. Why not then do this simple and easy thing, go down and wash in the Jordan. Almost as abruptly as he had turned his horses' heads away from Elisha's house, Naaman now turned their heads in the direction of the Jordan. I like to think it was not far from the place where one day the Young Man who was to heal the lepers, and by whose death all sinners can be cleansed, although sinless himself, went down into Jordan to be bap-

[175]

tized of John. There Naaman got out of his chariot and, divesting himself of his rich robes, stepped down into the dark waters of the narrow Jordan. According to the instructions of Elisha he dipped himself seven times. After the first time he looked at his arms and his legs, and there was no sign of a cure. He dipped himself twice, and it was the same. The third time, the fourth time, the fifth time, the sixth time, and still no change. But when he dipped himself the seventh time, and then looked at his body, lo, the leprosy was gone! His flesh had come again as the flesh of a little child!

Naaman was cured of his leprosy. But when you read the story you realize how he almost missed the cure, and narrowly escaped remaining a leper for the rest of his life by his foolish indulgence in anger when he went away in a rage from the house of Elisha, because Elisha had not come out in person to him but sent a servant to tell him to go down and wash in Jordan. Alas, how often men lose great possessions and great opportunities through an explosion of rage and anger! What wounds anger has inflicted! What husbands and wives it has separated! What chief friends it has alienated one from another! What churches it has blighted! When Jonah was disappointed at the repentance of Nineveh, and when the worm smote the gourd which had sprung up to shelter him from the fierce rays of the sun, he was very angry. But God said to him: "Doest thou well to be angry?" No man ever did well to be angry. And no one ever indulges himself in an angry rage without doing injury to others, and most of all to himself. When that elder brother in Christ's great tale came in from the fields that day, and saw the commotion about his father's house, and heard the music and the dancing, and, looking through the window, saw the table heaped with the feast for the celebration, and learned that it was in honor of the return of his prodigal brother, "he was angry, and would not go in." So anger keeps many a life from companionship and fellowship and joy.

GOD HELPS THOSE WHO HUMBLE THEMSELVES

Naaman was cured of his leprosy, but only when he put his pride and self-sufficiency aside. That is true of the disease of sin. God has a great cure for sin; but the terms are God's terms, not man's. Naaman had preconceptions as to how he was to be cured. "Behold," he said in effect, "I thought he would come out himself, and make a great ado over me, and call upon the name of his God, and pass his hands over my body, and thus cure me." So man has his own ideas as to the way he ought to be cured. John Bunyan names one of his characters Mr. Loth-to-Stoop. He was willing to come to terms with Emmanuel, provided Emmanuel recognized his own superior character and dignity. But when he found that there was no way to come to terms with Emmanuel except to bend the back and to stoop, he was hard put to it.

So far as rivers were concerned, Naaman was correct when he said: "Are not Abana and Pharpar . . . better than all the waters of Israel?" That is so. I can still distinctly see the clear waters of the river Abana, fresh from the snows of Hermon, as it flows into the city of Damascus; and I can still smell the sweet odors wafted by the winds from the gardens and groves of the villas along the banks of the Abana. Yes, Abana and Pharpar were better rivers than the dark and narrow Jordan; but there was one thing they could not do for Naaman: they could not cure leprosy. Only Jordan could do that.

We have today plenty of substitutes offered for the true

[177]

gospel of Christ, a gospel which requires us to wash and be clean. There is the so-called "Social Gospel," which in many churches has pushed the true gospel out altogether. There is the "Ethical Gospel," which tells men to be good, but does not give them the power to be good, and cannot help them when they fail to be good. And popular today are the "Racial Gospel," and the "International Gospel." All these, as far as they go, are good; but they cannot touch the disease of man's heart. They cannot reconcile him to God, or speak peace to his conscience.

In the seventeenth century Peter the Great, as a young man, visited London incognito. Two of the Society of Friends, learning who he was, presented him with a volume written by one of their number, hoping to acquaint him thus with the principles of the Friends. On the following Sabbath at their meeting house they saw two strangers enter. They were dressed in the usual garb of Englishmen, but they saw at once that they were none other than Peter the Great and his interpreter. As Peter took his seat among them, the Leader was speaking of Naaman and how he was cured of his leprosy only when he put aside his pride and went down into the River Jordan. Never imagining that Peter the Great had come in, the speaker said: "Though thou wast the greatest and mightiest among the kings and potentates of earth, thou art yet not too great to humble thyself before God and enter the Kingdom of God by the gate which he hath appointed, for into that Kingdom nothing that is unclean may enter." That is true. For all men, the greatest of earth and the humblest, the cure for sin is the same. And that cure is to bow at the foot of the cross and say: "God be merciful to me a sinner."

During World War I, the aged emperor of Austria-Hungary, who had ruled for more than sixty years, died.

According to the custom, this last of the Hapsburgs was carried to the gates of the gloomy crypt of the Church of the Capuchins in Vienna. When they knocked on the gate a voice from within called out: "Who is there?" Back came the answer: "His Serene Majesty, the Emperor of Austria." The voice within replied: "I know him not. Who is there?" Again the answer came back: "The Apostolic King of Hungary." Once more the voice within cried out: "I know him not. Who is there?" This time the answer came back: "Our brother Francis Joseph, a sinner." Then the gates opened and the emperor was laid among his fathers.

Calvary is the only cure for sin:

> There is a fountain filled with blood,
>   Drawn from Immanuel's veins;
> And sinners, plunged beneath that flood,
>   Lose all their guilty stains.

XVI

JUDAS—THE SON OF PERDITION

> "None of them is lost, but the son of perdition."
>

WE CAN BE SURE THAT ONE MAN OUT OF MANKIND HAS been saved, and we can be sure too that one soul out of mankind has been lost. We know this upon the authority of Jesus. He said of the penitent thief: "Today shalt thou be with me in paradise." Of Judas he said, speaking of his disciples in the great prayer he offered on the same night in which he was betrayed: "None of them is lost, but the son of perdition; that the scripture might be fulfilled."

The loss of a soul—and only Christ himself, who died to save sinners, has the authority to say who is saved and who is lost—the loss of an immortal soul is the supreme loss, the supreme tragedy. Jesus returns to that and warns us against it over and over again. He asked that great question: "What shall it profit a man, if he shall gain the whole world, and lose his own soul?" The loss of any soul is a tragedy; but that tragedy seems all the darker, the more solemn, when it is the soul of a man like Judas Iscariot, who was called to the highest office on earth, to be an apostle of Jesus Christ, who was associated closely with Jesus for the space of three years, and who had for a preacher, not the kind that you and I have, a fallible man of like passions with ourselves, but the living Word himself, the eternal Son of God. And yet Jesus, who died to save men, said that he was lost. "None of them is lost, but the son of perdition."

"The son of perdition"! Although he is one of the most sharply etched of the twelve disciples, Judas will ever be something of a mystery. His call to be an apostle; his avarice and covetousness; his yielding to the influence of the devil; his choosing Satan instead of Jesus after having been with Jesus for three years, and every day listening to his teaching and beholding the beauty of his spirit; the paltry price that he had asked for his treason; his remorse and repentance, his despair and suicide; in all this there is much that lies beyond the compass of our minds. When we read of his sin and crime we say that such a heinous sinner could not have suffered the remorse which Judas suffered; but when we come to the end of his story and read of his repentance and remorse, how he flung down the blood money before the priests and said: "I have sinned in that I have betrayed the innocent blood," we feel that his remorse is so great, and his repentance so sincere, that such a man could hardly have committed the crime attributed to him. So it is that there have been attempts to explain away the treason of Judas on the ground that he merely intended to precipitate Jesus into action by delivering him into the hands of his enemies, with the hope that he would then declare his kingship and take the throne of Israel, but never expected that he would be crucified and put to death; or again, that Judas, knowing the Scriptures, realized that someone must play the part of the traitor, and with a hero's courage volunteered to play that dreadful part. But if Judas were here, I am sure that he would repudiate such an explanation of what he did. When he went before the scribes and priests and Pharisees and flung down the blood money, what he confessed and lamented was not a mistake of judgment, or an error of conception and understanding of the person and work of Christ, but his sin. He said, "I have sinned in that I have betrayed the innocent blood."

THE MYSTERY OF GOD'S FOREKNOWLEDGE

The fact of God's foreknowledge and predestination and man's free will and responsibility is strikingly set forth in the tragedy of Judas. Jesus said of him: "The Son of Man indeed goeth, as it is written of him: but woe to that man by whom the Son of man is betrayed! Good were it for that man if he had never been born." In other words, Jesus said that his betrayal and crucifixion were a part of God's great plan for him and for the redemption of the world; and yet that the part which Judas played in the death of Jesus was so great a sin that it would have been better for him that he had never been born. Likewise Jesus said in his high priestly prayer: "Those that thou gavest me I have kept, and none of them is lost, but the son of perdition; that the scripture might be fulfilled." That, of course, does not mean that Judas was condemned and lost for the sake of fulfilling an Old Testament prediction, but rather that what he did had been foreknown and planned of God.

The Moslems have a tradition that at the Creation God set up great tablets five miles high, on which were inscribed all events between the Creation and the Day of Judgment, even to the movement of a leaf upon a tree. The doctrine of predestination, taught by itself, without the accompanying biblical doctrine of a personal freedom and accountability and responsibility, is a doctrine of fatalism, a dangerous and harmful doctrine, as is illustrated in the state of the Mohammedan world. But the Bible never teaches the doctrine of predestination by itself, but always together with the fact of man's freedom and responsibility. We are not puppets on the stage, moved to and fro by an invisible hand. We are not like balls rolled down a groove. We are not enmeshed by circumstances which make our course of action inevitable, but we have the freedom to choose what we shall do, and we are accountable for what we do.

This is a truth which is confirmed not only by Scripture, but by conscience. In the Bible these two truths are taught side by side: "A man's heart deviseth his way: but the Lord directeth his steps." "The lot is cast into the lap; but the whole disposing thereof is of the Lord." "Work out your own salvation, . . . for it is God which worketh in you both to will and to do of his good pleasure." The supreme illustration in the Bible, and in human history, of God's foreknowledge and determination, and at the same time man's freedom and accountability, is the crucifixion of Christ. Speaking on the Day of Pentecost to men who had had a part in that tragedy, Peter said: "Him, being delivered by the determinate counsel and foreknowledge of God, ye have taken, and by wicked hands have crucified and slain." There you have the death of Christ on the cross as a part of God's plan from before the foundation of the world for the redemption of mankind; and yet at the same time the wickedness and responsibility of the men who brought about his death on the cross. Likewise in the case of Judas, we have, upon the authority of Jesus, the statement that the betrayal of Christ into the hands of his enemies was a part of the appointed plan for the death of Christ for the sins of men; and yet, by the same authority, that Judas was responsible for what he had done. Satan, the Devil, John said, had "entered into him." "Have not I chosen you twelve, and one of you is a devil?" Jesus did not mean thereby that Judas was a demon, any more than Peter was, or any of the other disciples, but that he was yielding to the influence of Satan, and that under those circumstances, because his punishment would be so great, it had been better for him had he never been born. And Judas too realized his responsibility, and confessed his great transgression when he said: ''I have sinned in that I have betrayed the innocent blood.''

HOW MEN FALL SLOWLY

The tragedy of Judas tells us again how men fall slowly. Judas did not plunge in a moment into his great crime and transgression. It was the usual course that men follow before they go to their doom. He did not become a traitor in a day, or just in that night when he went out and met with the enemies of Jesus to betray him. That was only the last step. There is no reason to think that Judas was a traitor from the very beginning. Indeed, at that time there would have been no object in betraying Jesus, and none to whom he could have betrayed him, for then Jesus had no enemies and no marked opposition among the leaders of the people. John says that Jesus ''knew from the beginning'' who should betray him. But that does not mean that Judas was a traitor from the beginning, but only that Jesus foresaw what he would do. In the beginning of his relationship with Christ the prospect was as fair for Judas as for any of the other disciples.

Long ago in Florence an Italian painter was at work on a painting of the Madonna and Child. After much searching he selected a beautiful young peasant mother and her child as the model for the Virgin Mother of Jesus. Many years later he was at work on a study of Judas Iscariot. In search of a suitable model he visited prisons and penitentiaries, and at length in one of the jails found a man of sinister countenance and with a long record of heinous crimes, and chose him for his model. He came every day to the prison and set up his easel before this prisoner's cell. One day, as the painting was nearing completion, he saw that this condemned and wicked criminal was the very person whom, as a child, he had taken as the model for his painting of Mary and the infant Jesus! Great indeed are the possibilities for good and evil in every human soul!

In some Judæan village Judas first heard Jesus preach. His words stirred him and moved him, and he took other opportunities to see him and hear him. One day Jesus turned to him, as he had done with the other disciples, and said to Judas, "Follow me," and Judas arose and left all and followed him. When Jesus looked into his face that day he saw in him a possible apostle. We cannot tell how or why it was; but whereas in the case of the other disciples, their association with Jesus brought out the best that was in them, the association of Judas with Jesus brought out the worst that was in him. The same sun nourishes the weeds and brings out the flowers. So Christ, as Paul said, is a "savour of life unto life," or "of death unto death." Through the choice of his own will, and through his obedience to or his rejection of the Holy Spirit, a man is either better or worse because of his association with Christ.

Much in the tragedy and fall of Judas is beyond our scrutiny. Yet there is also some light thrown upon this mystery. One motive, according to the gospels, was that of avarice. John said that Judas objected to Mary's beautiful and costly gift, when she broke the alabaster box of ointment, precious, very costly, and poured it on the feet of Jesus, because "he was a thief, and had the bag," He thought the money ought to have been spent on the poor;

but his purpose was to get it into the bag and take it for himself. But John is writing after the event, and no doubt did not know at the time that Judas was a thief. That in-cident in conection with Mary's gift to Jesus was probably the last step in his covetousness. The first time he stole from the bag he probably intended to return the small amount he had taken. But he repeated his transgression, un-til now he sank so low as to be distressed and hurt at the thought of so much being "wasted" on Mary's ointment, and which he might have had for himself. Avarice was consummated in hypocrisy. Judas cared not for the poor, but he wanted the money for himself.

It is quite likely too that disappointment with Jesus, because he did not declare himself a king and take an earthly throne, played its part in the final downfall of Judas. He was not the only one of the disciples who thought that his association with Jesus was to make him share in the riches and glory of an earthly kingdom. But the others survived that disappointment. Judas did not. It may well have been that resentment and the spirit of revenge also contributed to the fall of Judas. His conscience must have let him know, when he listened to the preaching of Jesus, that Jesus knew what was in his heart, as when he said on one occasion, "Beware of covetousness," and again, "One of you is a devil." Having made up his mind to desert Jesus and betray him, and get what little he could out of it, he did it in a way that brought, as he thought at the time, a grim satisfaction to him. There were other ways in which Judas could have pointed out Jesus to his enemies that night when he betrayed him. But he chose to do it with the beautiful symbol of friendship and confidence, and betrayed him with a kiss! That would indicate that the light that was in Judas had become darkness, and that he

JUDAS—THE SON OF PERDITION

sought satisfaction in delivering Jesus over to his enemies "with a kiss."

But we have not mentioned the real explanation of the fall of Judas, and that is the explanation given us by John and by Jesus in the Gospels, the explanation of every soul's transgression and sin and fall. Luke says that Satan entered into Judas, and John says that the devil put it into the heart of Judas to betray him. All these other things that we have mentioned—avarice, covetousness, jealousy, disappointment, revenge—were only baits used by Satan. As between Satan and Jesus, Judas finally chose Satan. He refused to let Christ come into him, and opened the door to Satan. And there you have the whole history of evil, of temptation, and of a lost soul. The great Russian writer Dostoevski, in his remarks on Satan, says that there are two things that Satan desires above all others to accomplish: First, to reduce all men to the same level, without spiritual character and spiritual aspirations; and second, to persuade all men that Satan is not a reality. Beware of that! If you make Satan a myth, you may wake up one day to discover that you yourself are a myth.

MEN FALL IN SPITE OF WARNINGS

The tragedy of Judas tells us how men are lost in spite of warnings and in spite of the obstacles which God sets before them. Judas had many warnings. It was early in their association that Jesus, speaking one day to the disciples, said: "Have I not chosen you twelve, and one of you is a devil?" Every time he heard Jesus utter, as he so often did, searching words as to covetousness and the love of money, that was a warning for Judas. When Jesus told men to cut off the right hand or the right foot or to pluck out the right eye, and go maimed into eternal life rather than with their whole body to be cast into hell, that was a warning for Judas. When he said, "Remember Lot's wife," that warned Judas of the fate of those who start to follow him and turn back. Then there was a warning of a different nature, a tender and a beautiful appeal. When Judas found fault with Mary's beautiful gift of that precious ointment, Jesus praised Mary and said she had done this against the day of his burial, and then added those touching words: "The poor always ye have with you; but me ye have not always." Hard indeed by this time must have been the heart of Judas to resist such an appeal! Then came the night of the Last Supper. Event after event on that memorable night was an appeal and a warning to Judas. First, when Jesus said to them, "One of you shall betray me." And what an appeal, and what a warning that was too, when Jesus, as he made the circle of the disciples with that towel and that basin in his hand, washed the feet of Judas! What did Judas think when he felt the touch of those hands upon his feet, and when he gave him the sop and said to him, "That thou doest, do quickly"? Perhaps that too was a final appeal. And when, in the Garden of Gethsemane, after Judas had bestowed that traitorous kiss upon him, Jesus said to him: "Judas, betrayest thou the Son of man with a kiss?" Perhaps that too was a final appeal; and even then, had Judas turned and repented Christ would have forgiven him. But over all these warnings and over all these obstacles Judas rushed onward to his doom. He went out, "and it was night." And what a night it was! A night that separated him from his better self, from the eleven disciples, and from Jesus himself. When Balaam, another gifted man who betrayed his soul for the sake of gain, was riding eagerly on his ass towards Moab to win a reward for cursing the children of

Israel, an angel with a drawn sword appeared in his path. So God sends angels, warnings, obstacles, pleadings, to hold us back from doing evil. When you see the flash of that angel's sword do not attempt to pass it.

HOW MEN CHOOSE THEIR OWN PLACE AND DESTINY

Finally, the tragedy of Judas tells us how men choose their own place and destiny. After the ascension of Jesus, Peter assembled the disciples and a hundred and twenty friends of Jesus, and called on them to appoint a successor to Judas. He spoke of the fall of Judas and his tragic end, and how he was a guide to them that took Jesus. Before the lot was cast to choose between Joseph and Matthias as a successor to Judas, Luke says they all prayed that God would make the lot his own choice. But since a hundred and twenty could hardly pray all together, there is little doubt that Peter made the prayer. And this is what he said: "Thou, Lord, which knowest the hearts of all men, show whether of these two thou hast chosen, that he may take part of this ministry and apostleship, from which Judas by transgression fell, that he might go to his own place."

To his own place! What noble and tender restraint there was on the part of Peter when he put it that way! Remembering his own base denial, Peter does not denounce his fellow disciple Judas, but says only that he went "to his own place." Judas was called of God and of Christ to the highest of all places, to be an apostle of Jesus Christ. And when you see Judas going out that night to betray Jesus, remember that Jesus once said to him, "Follow me." He called him to the highest place, and had Judas yielded his heart to Christ, sermons would be preached on Judas today like the sermons which are preached on John and Peter and Philip and Paul. God calls all of us to the highest place, to be a redeemed child of God. When Saul was amazed at what Samuel told him, that he had been chosen to be king over Israel, Samuel said to him: "On whom is all the desire of Israel? Is it not on thee?" The same words God speaks through his Holy Spirit to all of us. He calls you to the highest place.

Men choose their final place; but they also choose their place in this life. Before Judas chose his final place he had chosen a place in this life which determined that future place. These present years that we live are a part of our destiny. Even in this life we see strange contrasts in personality and in character, in happiness and in influence, in hope and in memory, because men have chosen so differently. Hence, every day we are passing on the street those who have been traitors to their soul because they have made the wrong choice. How important that choice is! Every morning, when the sun calls you out of slumber, resolve in your heart to choose the best and highest life for that one day. That is a most illuminating phrase of Paul where he tells us how he made his choice, how he pressed toward the mark of the prize of the high calling of God in Christ Jesus: "If that I may apprehend that for which also I am apprehended of Christ Jesus." In other words, he bent every effort to reach that place which Christ had chosen for him and to which he had called him. Not only for this life but for the world to come, men choose their own place. Jesus said to his disciples: "I go to prepare a place for you, . . . that where I am, there ye may be also." But Judas chose in preference "his own place." And what a place that was! A place away from God and away from Christ. Even at the very last, had Judas turned with tears to Christ as Peter did, he would have been forgiven; and after his resurrection Jesus might have made a special appearance to Judas as he did to Peter. But Judas did not turn. He went out, "and it was night."

For myself, when I read this story of the tragedy and fall of Judas, and then search my own heart, and when I remember that I am a man of like passions with Judas, and how Satan desires to have me and enter into me, and how men are beguiled and deceived by the temptations of this world, and for the sake of the visible give up the invisible and betray their soul, then I feel that the only thing for me to say is what the disciples said that night, one by one, when Jesus told them that that night one of them should betray him, "Lord, is it I?"